Learning to Ride as an Adult

Learning to Ride as an Adult

A New Training Method for First-Time Riders

by

Erika Prockl

Copyright of first edition © 2003 by Cadmos Equestrian

Copyright of this edition © 2006 by Cadmos Equestrian

First published as *Wenn Erwachsene in den Sattel wollen* by Cadmos Verlag in 1998

Translated by Kostanze Allsopp

Typesetting and design: Ravenstein, Verden

Illustrations: Gabriele Wagner

Photographs: Josef Puchinger

Printed in Germany

ISBN 3-86127-908-8

Contents

Introduction

I was already almost twenty-five years old when I decided I wanted to learn to ride. As I was relatively athletic, I did not think that my age would be a problem – how wrong I was! To begin with, the not uncommon riding school practice of screaming instructors unnerved me quite badly, and I found to my disappointment that I was making no progress at all. I never really felt "at home" on a horse and came very close to giving up riding altogether.

The majority of riders learn to ride as children or during adolescence, and therefore have never encountered the glass wall of insecurity and fear which can encircle the adult riding student and which turns a normal person into an awkward clumsy fool, unable to hear instructions. Accordingly, most riders have little understanding of the adult novice's problems.

I, on the other hand, can well remember how helpless and unsupported I felt.

Fluid, confident riding can only be achieved through practice. But more than that, the adult learner must first unlearn habits of bad posture and gain an insight into balance and coordination of the body. Only after learning not to fight a constant battle against one's own clumsy body, can the rider learn to understand and work with the horse.

This book is intended to offer you the opportunity to practice riding movements in your own time and in familiar surroundings, without stress or hindrance. These movements can then be joined together into more complex coordinated movements and finally be put into practice on the horse.

Erika Prockl

Erika Prockl

Battling with the urge to cling on

Anybody who wants to learn to ride as an adult will have to be prepared to do battle with failure. Even from those very first hours on a horse, when any notion of a feeling of unity with the horse will seem eons away, when the motion, strongly reminiscent of an earthquake, tips the beginner off-balance, every part of the body tenses up and, to increase the misery, the riding instructor keeps on insisting that the rider should loosen up and start relaxing.

Of course, the rider would gladly comply, but his/her body isn't cooperating. As soon as the rider sits in the saddle and everything below him begins to move violently, the rider becomes a **clinging monkey** – an uninspiring occurrence.

The muscle groups on the inside of the upper thigh, the upper and lower leg, the knees, the buttocks and, of course, the hands, close in reflex – everything is needed to hold on and stay on.

This is an involuntary act as well as an unwanted one, because it is impossible to simply switch off reflexes and the instinct to survive.

At the walk, our beginner is able to follow the instructions of the riding teacher up to a point. At the trot and canter, everything simply falls apart. In order to keep his students, the riding instructor will remain polite, but it is easy to see that his enthusiasm for this kind of student is limited.

Other riders seem to be floating effortlessly on their horses. Children and adolescents provocatively demonstrate how simple and enjoyable riding can be. Are these people all naturally talented?

They are not, and our beginner is not as untalented as it seems at first glance. Adult

learners, however, no longer have all the *prerequisites* that are imperative for riding:

- a highly developed sense of balance
- good body control, including of muscles and joints that are rarely used from day to day, as well as the ability to have equal agility on both sides of the body
- nonchalance or courage, whatever one may call it
- love and understanding of animals, combined with a practically unlimited trust in one's partner, the horse.

Children who are *physically active* are ideal riding students. They still have all the prerequisites and can learn complicated movement sequences in play by means of imitation. Due to the fact that they imitate quite uncritically, it can, however, happen that they imitate every bit of nonsense. Therefore, children always only ride as well as they are taught. "Couch potatoes," who spend their leisure time without much physical activity, watching television and playing on computers, are noticeably clumsy and, as a result, fearful.

When you have had the opportunity of learning to ride at a very young age, you will find it difficult to imagine the problems which novice adult riders face.

9

In the case of **adolescents**, unfortunately, physical fitness is no longer a foregone conclusion. A residue of the natural childhood ability to balance will remain, and this ensures that the inhibiting factor of fear can more easily be overcome. Lack of physical movement and the habit of spending leisure time in unhealthy ways, however, have already left their mark. Often, their general daily posture is completely wrong, namely drooping and sluggish. Thus, it is very difficult to impart corrections of the seat and posture.

An **adult** has forgotten to a large degree the art of balancing his body. His control of his body is also built upon well-known movement sequences, carried out repeatedly. During childhood we are able to learn new types of movement by means of imitation. From the onset of puberty, we lose this ability and have to combine new movements with movement patterns already memorized by our brains. If you have had an active childhood, you will be able to select from a large number of types of movement. If, on the other hand, your childhood was spent just sitting around, any type of sports activity will be fairly difficult to learn.

It is essential that an adult should be taught in a completely different way to children or adolescents. As he is unable to learn in play, i.e., via imitation, he needs to be able to think through every course of a movement in peace, in order to be able to consciously memorize every detail. He needs explanations, many exercises which he can carry out at his own pace, and sufficient time to combine the different movement sequences.

An excellent instruction aid to correct the seat is lungeing lessons. Unfortunately they are often given by helpful but unqualified aides, and in some cases this form of riding lesson actually does more harm than good.

It was l'Hotte, the French "Riding Pope," who quite rightly said: "In the art of equitation, knowing a great amount is just the beginning to acquire a good elemental knowledge."

So far, riding has not become a popular mass sport, but even so, you should not expect the undivided attention of a good riding instructor – at least not if you are only paying the average price for a riding lesson.

If you want to achieve something in this sport, despite the odds against it, there is only one approach: the do-it-yourself method. Read books on equitation, observe good riders, and first and foremost get your own body back in shape.

If adolescents between the age of 14 and 19 are asked to stand on only one leg, 56 percent prefer the left leg. If the leg they are standing on is changed, around 50 percent of 14-year-olds felt slightly insecure. In the case of 19-year-olds, 75 percent already show a preference for their favorite leg.

This means that the ability to keep one's balance diminishes fairly rapidly with age,

Horses are immediately able to recognize the expertise of their rider.

Exercise 1:
Improvement of Balance
and Equal Dexterity of Both Sides

Imitate a stork during numerous possible activities and use only one leg as support. This makes your position unstable and your sense of balance will be mobilized. Your morning activities in the bathroom are as good a start as any.

Change legs. You will soon find out that you have a favourite leg to stand on. When you first sit on a horse, the different parts of your body will initially also behave with very different levels of dexterity, and it will take a lot of work to balance this as much as you can.

Walk on pavement curbs as you used to do as a child; use everything that imitates a gymnastics bar as a training aid. Maybe you can even secretly visit a children's playground when taking the dog for its evening walk – there are many opportunities to reawaken your sense of balance!

whereas the one-sidedness increases in equal measure.

As a right- or left-handed person, you are aware that you are distinctly more dextrous with one hand than with the other. However, do you also know which is your more skilled leg and which is the clumsy one?

The secret of perfect riding lies in having completely relaxed buttocks. Relaxed buttocks, however, will only come when you have a good sense of balance. We now have to attempt to shrink the area of support you require through daily exercises. This will reawaken your dormant sense of balance and will, at the same time, exercise your body control and equalize dexterity of both sides.

When we sit down, we generally choose as comfortable and stable a seat as possible. This changes with a horse. However inviting a saddle may look, it is only suited for comfortable relaxation if it is used as a bar stool. On a horse, we balance with our buttocks on a part of the arched back of the

Exercise 2: Motion while sitting.

horse – if our horse is going forward correctly. This means that we only have a very small support area, which, to make things even more difficult, is moving violently. Therefore, it is important to become re-accustomed to sitting in motion.

Go out and buy a **physiotherapy ball** (often called a space hopper). This is a slightly larger version of a gymnastics ball.

You can buy these inflatable balls in several sizes in most specialist orthopaedic shops. Normally a ball with a diameter of 75 cm is the ideal size. If you are very tall, choose the 85 cm size, and if you are short, go for 65 cm.

Such a ball will cost no more than the equivalent of a couple of riding lessons, and you will soon realize that this is a really sound investment.

Exercise 2:
Sitting in Motion

Take every chance you can to sit on your physio-ball. It is impossible to sit completely still, without any action at all, as you have to find your balance anew all the time. Don't hunch up your back, sit upright. The ball almost gives you the feeling of sitting on a living being, and you should increase this feeling by continuously bouncing the ball up and down.

Even Granddad now likes to sit in motion.

Not only is this an excellent preparation for riding, it also acts as a pronounced relief for tensed-up back muscles.

To begin with, it is possible that you will find sitting in motion quite strenuous. In this case, simply change to solid seating and back to sitting in motion. Allocate your ball a place next to your sofa. After a long and stressful day at work, sitting in front of the television all evening is possibly not the ideal way to relax the body. Instead, you should switch to the ball at intervals.

ful situations, and the less forceful the urge will become and the less often it will strike. Even the best rider will from time to time experience the urge to tense up and cling to their horse!

The rider is continually displaced. It requires a good sense of balance to be able to correct one's seat immediately. The ball is an excellent instrument to use for training one's sense of balance.

You will soon experience progress on horseback, because you will be less tensed up. The urge to cling on, however, may accompany you for the rest of your riding years. Sad but true.

The more experienced you become, the more you will be able to confront stress-

Upright is out, relaxed is in

Now we shall come to a typical problem of civilization. We sit for too long and in most cases adopt a poor position as well. Walking is healthy; relaxed standing can just about be justified. Sitting ceaselessly, however, leads to a weak posture, in other words, overstretching and slackening of the muscular system. Sitting is particularly unhealthy if it is carried out

• over long periods
• immobile
• in extreme positions.

Our spine has a natural S-shaped curvature. This shape gives the back stability and flexibility, and should be retained at all times. If we twist our spine for a short period, this will create a significant increase inpressure on our intervertebral discs, the buffer zones between the vertebrae, but a healthy spine is perfectly able to endure some short-term overstrain. If we sit in a tensed up incorrect posture for hours, this will have long-term negative effects.

Many years ago, only two types of sitting positions were known: the **working posture** and the listening posture. The working posture is a continuous slightly forward hunched position. From very early youth onward – due to the fact that we encounter level tables and desks almost everywhere – we have to work for hours in this posture, although this can wear out our discs significantly.

The listening posture is an upright type of sitting down, during which a supporting backrest is intended to relieve the strain put on our spine. Unfortunately, it is rarely possible to take up this healthier posture in a normal working day.

In the past, children and adolescents were always admonished to sit straight: "Sit

When hacking out, the rider should sit upright in a flexible position. A slumped weak position puts avoidable stress on the forelegs of the horse and is damaging for the rider's spine.

straight – hold your head up" was the usual rule. Nowadays, this admonishment is basically treated as a joke, and this has encouraged an unhealthy modern variant of the sitting posture: *slack and languid.*

In this relaxed type of sitting position, the back is rounded in such an extreme way that the natural bend of the spine disappears completely. This imposes great pressure on each disc.

Anybody sitting in a hunched up position ...   *... will do the same on horseback.*

Not only has this unhealthy posture success-fully taken over schools and offices, but it has also become the preferred mode for spending hours and hours in front of the television.

If this seemingly comfortable posture is kept up for some time, the back muscles will lengthen due to overstretching. At the same time, the muscles of the chest area are short-ened to such a degree that the pectoral girdle is forced to be carried tilted in a forward posture. Now, it is really only a matter of time as to when the strain will lead to illness. It is very difficult to convince a "relaxed" person that not only does this amount to complete stupidity, but also that it is only a matter of time until he has dam-aged his spine beyond repair.

Years of faulty posture change the body to such a degree that an upright posture feels uncomfortable to the person in question.

Let us now look at this aspect from a riding point of view. Luckily, on a horse we have to sit completely upright, or we would otherwise hinder our horse as well as ourselves. This means that we will have to practise the healthy upright seat constantly during our daily routines. This means that it will be available under the more difficult situation on a horse. Before we start the difficult work of consciously practising the sitting upright posture, we need to think again very carefully about the advantages of the upright seat on a horse:

- With his weight, the rider impairs the freedom of movement of the horse. If this weight also wobbles around, the horse has to find its balance all the time to cope with the unstable load. If the rider, on the other hand, sits on the horse **in balance**, he impairs the horse far less through his movements.
- The rider feels the movement of the horse's back as a constant up and down under his buttocks. The rider **swings** in tune with this tempo. This **movement of the rider in harmony** with the horse can only be achieved in the upright posture.
- Due to the constant change of movement, riding has a positive effect on the back. Provided the rider sits in an **upright posture**, the movements of the back and abdominal muscles, which can be likened to a pumping and massage motion, are beneficial to the spine.

Let us now start to achieve this new upright posture. Any chair that is hard enough can serve as a horse. It is far more difficult to straighten up correctly on soft, unstable buttocks. Therefore you should practise on a chair to begin with.

Later, when you have established a more or less stable upright posture, you will easily be able to achieve the same on the physioball.

About the spine

If we sit up too quickly and too sharply from our hunched-up position, in line with the saying "Push out your chest," we only activate the long back muscles for a short period of time; we are incapable of maintaining this tension for any length of time. Even without the equine "antagonist action," we would soon slump back into the familiar sloppy posture. On the horse itself, such a sudden straightening up is completely useless, as the first faster strides at the trot will lead this tensed up posture to collapse. And as far as the canter goes, leave that to the imagination!

Both sides of the backbone are supported by massive deep-seated muscles that are responsible for the stability of the entire spine. Added to that are short muscles which in each case only connect two adjacent vertebrae. On the surface are additional muscles,

mainly running at a slant, which cover the back. Which muscle group can help us to sit upright all of the time?

Ismacogy was developed in Vienna, by Professor Anne Seidel. It is concerned with the constant tensing and relaxing of the muscles. Ismacogy is an extremely practical

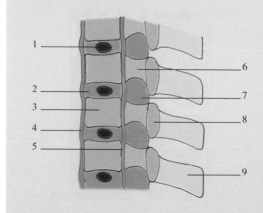

Structure of the spine
1. Pulposus
2. Intervertebral discs
3. Body of a vertebra
4. Abdominal longitudinal band
5. Dorsal longitudinal band
6. and 7. Vertebral canal
8. Vertebral arch
9. Spine of a vertebra

This posture is damaging not only for the rider's spine, but also for the horse.

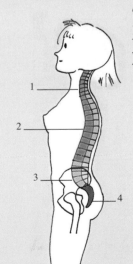

Our "vertebral" inside:
1. *Seven cervical vertebrae*
2. *Twelve thoracic vertebrae*
3. *Five lumbar vertebrae*
4. *Sacrum and coccyx*

and especially discreet type of training method for our professional life, dominated by sitting. With the help of Professor Seidel's ismacogy, we shall now attempt to learn to sit up properly, maintain an upright position, and adopt this posture as often as we can in our daily life. Only once it has been sufficiently developed, can we hope to retain it on a horse under more difficult conditions.

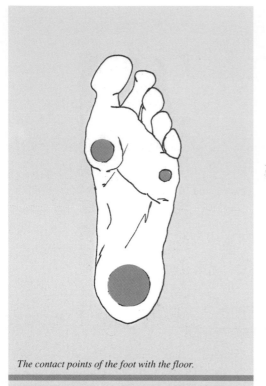

The contact points of the foot with the floor.

The floor contact points sitting on the horse.

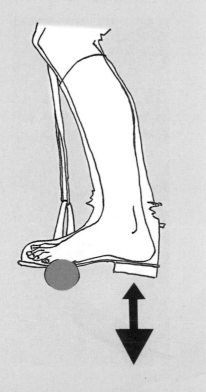

Exercise 3:
Acquiring an Upright Position

On the chair: Sit barefoot on the edge of a hard chair. The thighs should not rest on the chair but instead should form a right angle with the lower legs. The heels of the feet should be closer together than the front of the feet – in other words, in a slight V-shape. The feet make contact with the floor via three points:

- the heel-bone
- the ball of the foot
- the ball of the little toe.

We put a load on these three contact points, but it is not necessary to ram them onto the floor with force. In the same way, we must not push ourselves down in the stirrup – we should only keep contact consciously. The heel contact point on the horse is translated into the springing downward movement of the joint. Therefore, we have the same "contact with the floor" as in the buttocks.

Maintaining these floor contact points results in the buildup of mounting tension, an upward pull in the calf, which runs via the upper side of the upper thigh and can eventually be felt in the lower region of the abdomen. We now make use of this tension, starting from the bottom, to begin setting each vertebra upright on the one below. This is not as easy as it sounds, as there is a risk, especially in the lower region, of hollowing the back.

The sacrum vertebrae have fused together to form one bone. This is a good thing, because we will have intimate contact with the ground more often than we like to think.

In the lumbar area, the fifth lumbar vertebra, which has to cushion the movements of the pelvis against the spine, is particularly prone to excessive strain. It is difficult to stabilize this extremely mobile area without compromising its flexibility.

Sitting upright is now achieved via the thoracic spine. You will have found out, or find out now, that straightening up cannot be achieved if the thoracic girdle in the front hangs downward like an incorrectly carried shoulder bag. The thoracic girdle is supposed to be in its correct position on the back!

The head has significant weight. Therefore, it should be carried free and balanced. In order to achieve that, we, metaphorically speaking, try to lengthen the cervical spine so that the head can grow upward from the shoulders. Head, throat, and chin must form a ninety-degree angle.

Now, with the upper arms hanging down straight and relaxed, the lower arms are laid very lightly on the upper thighs, the inside of the palms facing upward.

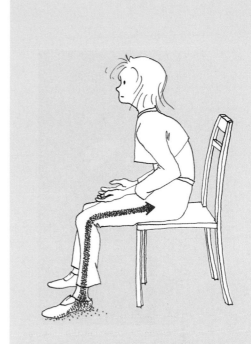

Exercise 3.1: The beginning of learning to sit upright.

Exercise 3.2: Each vertebra is upright in perfect position.

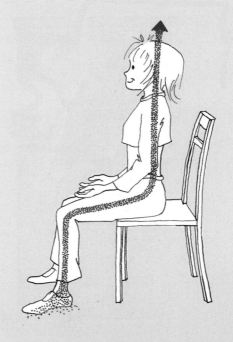

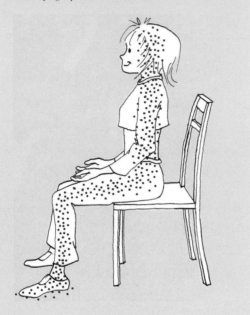

Exercise 3.3: The tension is diminished, but the upright position remains intact.

In the beginning, when sitting on a horse, we will be continuously occupied with straightening up and the build-up of tension because even the slightest unusual movement will upset our balance. However, even experienced riders continually need to improve their posture – it is simply an essential part of riding.

In this kind of straightening up, the toes should always remain freely mobile – they should be able to play. This playing of the toes, which every baby does with abandon, is something that we adults have almost forgotten to do, due to pinching and wrongly fitting shoes. Wriggling the large toe, for example, can help the leg build up its extensor tension. However, it can only do this, if it has sufficient freedom of movement. Therefore, comfortable shoes or boots that allow the toes sufficient space are important.

Now we are in **balance** and are able to release a large part of the muscular tension that helped us attain this position without losing our balance. As chairs can neither walk around nor buck, this will be a simple accomplishment for us.

Wrong on every chair

"Slim and narrow" is the current fashion trend for women. Moreover, women are used to keeping their legs closely together from an early age. Men, on the other hand, have the freedom to choose a more comfortable posture.

On the inside of our upper thighs run the so-called adductors. These muscle groups have the task, among others, of closing the legs. They react automatically to pressure and touch. This fast closure was probably very practical when our hairy ancestors were still swinging from one tree to the next. When we start riding, we are going to encounter a lot of problems with these muscle groups, because this closure in a flash happens when our balance becomes unstable and will repeatedly lead us to cling and press our legs together. Horses will either feel this pressure on their back and

flank muscles as a pain or, at least, as an uncomfortable sensation. On the other hand, this automatic closure of the adductors can help to keep you sitting on the horse when it bucks or after a misjudged jump. Everything has its positive and negative sides.

It is important to stretch all muscle groups on the inside of the upper thighs and then to relax them, so that we can sit down comfortably in a *broad seat* and so that our horse does not feel impaired by a single hard muscle strand. A horse with a narrow conformation causes fewer problems; a broad, well-nourished animal, on the other hand, pushes the legs and the seat of the rider farther apart.

Stretching only the inside of the upper thighs is not enough. The horse's propelling force is situated in its hindquarters. What is the use of relatively loosened up legs if the hard, tensed up muscles of the buttocks

Anybody who wants to ride needs to be able to stretch.

block the movements that are coming from the horse's hindquarters! Our buttocks and seat also need to become relaxed and broad – they need to flow apart. This is an even less accustomed posture than simply the opened legs.

Exercise 4:
The Broad Seat

Seat yourself on a chair the wrong way around to create consciously a new, unaccustomed seating posture. Place yourself in a correct upright position. Initially, stretch the inside of the upper thighs, the adductors, and then relax these muscle groups. Now concentrate on broadening and then completely relaxing the muscles of the buttocks, which, just like the legs, we normally keep close together in our daily life. We automatically sit this way on a very familiar seat. Now it is time to practise it on your chair. Your knees should remain relaxed throughout.

The broad seat on the ball: If you have already become accustomed to the new type of seat on the chair, start using it on the physio-ball. Always ensure that you do not hollow your back during this exercise!

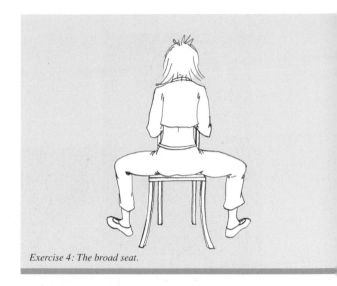

Exercise 4: The broad seat.

The broad seat on the horse.

You will find that the broad seat is a posture that really needs getting used to. It is understandable that in the beginning you will not be able to maintain it on the horse under more difficult conditions.

If we sit in complete relaxation, the horse will experience the soft and relaxed muscles of the buttocks and the relaxed touch of the legs of the rider simply as a massage, not as an oppression. Soft, relaxed rider's legs do not

If you get tired lean against the armrest of a sofa or a soft armchair.
Stretch your abductors in this position.

impair the movement of the flanks, nor do they interfere with the breathing of the horse.

"The rider should keep his lower thighs in constant contact with the horse, and will find that this occurs naturally if he lets them hang down naturally and does not have to search for contact by means of a forced posture of the calves." (Steinbrecht)

All commands such as: "The points of the toes toward the horse!" or "The points of the toes should be turned inward!" or "Heels down!" forcibly lead to the legs being in a cramped position. Relaxed legs, on the other hand, lead automatically to an almost parallel position of the feet and allow the heels to come down.

Take up the broad seat as often as you can. It's ideal to watch television that way. You can assume that you will be able to maintain the broad seat on a horse in difficult situations only after this position has become completely familiar.

5

Different people tense up differently

Ongoing stress, in other words, overstraining, can lead to chronic tension, which occurs predominantly in certain parts of the body, depending on the person. The cool mathematician, the analysing type will have problems in the lumbar region. This is the area where he blocks off anything unpleasant. The creative and artistic type is particularly predisposed to tension in the neck and shoulders.

All people, irrespective of their type, however, have the tendency to tense up in the area of the neck and shoulders.

The movement of the horse means that the seat base of the rider is continuously moving up and down. Even when we are lifted up by the horse, we react with the slightest reflex-like tensing of the muscles of the seat and buttocks. This is intensified even more when we are shot up or pushed up. A horse that is unwilling to work has all these unpleasant reactions in its repertoire. We tense up even more in the area of the neck and shoulders, because any feeling of insecurity leads to a blockage in this area. Once this area stiffens up, our hands will become hard and unresponsive. Thus, the tension that the rider experiences can attack from the top and bottom at the same time and will thus block other parts of the body in a split second.

We can only consciously relax and release our tension when the horse lowers its back. The deeper we sit in the horse, the more we will feel contact and security, and the easier it will be for us to relax.

For each rider, experienced or novice, riding is an exchange between reflex-like tensing up and conscious relaxation.

When the horse's back pushes up, the experienced rider will only react with a minute tensing up – it is impossible to completely switch off reflexes. After years of practice, the rider will relax automatically when the horse lowers its back, in perfect rhythm and without the slightest effort, so that the rider will barely notice it.

The inexperienced rider, on the other hand, will suffer greatly. The speed between the changeover from tensing up and relaxing places excessive demands on the rider, and the result is an uncontrolled sum of tensions, which the horse understandably does not appreciate.

Therefore, in order to learn to react with greater speed, we will have to practice relaxing continuously. Even your place of work can be an ideal training area for these exercises. The stiff work posture that we assume when we are sitting in front of a computer, for example, the concentrated observing from a constant distance in a constant direction, is very similar to the tensed-up posture on a horse. And by the way, a long evening in front of the television has the same negative effect!

Perfectly normal types of day-to-day tension buildup.

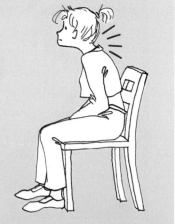

Exercise 5:
Relaxation by Means
of Conscious Thought

In this exercise, **stare** consciously at an object. At the same time place your hand on the base of your neck muscles, or in other words, on your hairline. Feel your way down along the muscle. Can you feel how rigid these muscles are?

Let your hand fall down, close and relax your eyes. Consciously push all unpleasant thoughts away. At the same time, breathe out audibly.

Now consciously **think** your way to the base of the neck muscles and try to relax and loosen up in this area. Consciously thinking of relaxation of a body part is the simplest way of relaxing individual parts of the body. It does, however, require a certain ability to aim your thoughts in the required direction.

Exercise 6:
Relaxation by Means
of the Circling Shower

If your exclusively mental relaxing process isn't quite working as it should be yet, you might try the trick with the shower: simply imagine you are standing under a nice, warm shower. The spray massages you with small circling move-

The rider's tension are transfered immediately.

ments – a gorgeous feeling! Place your hand back on your neck. Can you feel how much softer your muscles are now?

You should also practise these relaxation exercises on the physio-ball. The up-and-down movements of the ball are very similar to the up-and-down movements of the horse's back. Therefore, these relaxation exercises can be practised with great effect.

Always keep in mind that the blood circulation is optimized in a relaxed muscle: in other words, tight muscles are not sufficiently supplied with blood. Muscles that are under constant tension suffer from lack of blood circulation, on the one hand, and on the other, waste materials cannot be

removed, which can lead to painful cramps. To begin with, every relaxation process takes a long time and requires a high degree of concentration. With increased familiarity with the process, you will feel it become easier and more pleasant.

If you find yourself two feet above the back of your horse as a result of a faster movement on the part of your horse, you can rest assured that your muscles are extremely tight. Search out your tight muscles. Localize them and relax them time and time again.

It is not usually possible to eliminate tension from our stress-filled working environment. Once you have learned to relax your neck and shoulder muscles, however, you will find that it also enormously profits your daily life.

The slipped thoracic girdle

There is absolutely no point in sitting down "correctly" before a riding lesson and expecting that this situation is going to last for any great period of time. Due to the forceful movements that the base of the seat has to endure, our upright posture will collapse again and again. We become more hunched up with every step, the thoracic girdle slips forward more and more. One little bit and another little bit, and before we know it we are back to our old, familiar incorrect posture and never even noticed the change.

As we are used from childhood to writing and reading in an incorrect, hunched up position on incorrect (i.e., level, rather than sloping) tables, the slipping forward of the thoracic girdle has become an accepted posture. This part of the body, which enjoys nothing more than rambling, rests on the thorax, held in place only by muscles. This is extremely

practical where agility is concerned, but impractical if we are having to contend with the strong up-and-down movements on the back of a horse. Due to our insecurity, we not only tighten the muscles of the neck and shoulders, but we also tilt the thoracic girdle forward. This forms part of the hunched up position, a protective posture that we first learned to take up in our mother's womb. If we want to ride in a relaxed manner and in balance with the horse, we need to say good-bye to this everyday incorrect posture.

Exercise 7:
Moving the Thoracic Girdle Back

Sit down in a relaxed position with splayed-out buttocks on a chair or on the ball. Then establish floor contact and start sitting in an upright posture, vertebra by vertebra, beginning from the bottom.

Now pull up your shoulders in the direction of your ears and then let them sink backward in a relaxed motion. This exercise helps you ensure that the thoracic girdle is restored to its correct place.

If you find this posture strange, or even unpleasant, to begin with, then you can be assured that your pectoral muscles have been shortened by quite a bit. Do not mistake the natural sinking down of the thoracic girdle with the military-like stiff "Chest up and out." Unfortunately, this command can still be heard in many riding schools.

Dagmar is sitting in a correct position.

Exercise 7: Move back the thoracic girdle.

31

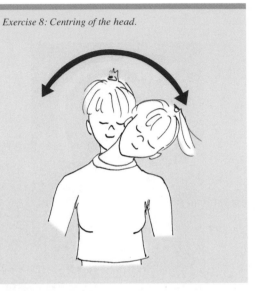

Exercise 8: Centring of the head.

down toward your right shoulder; then your left ear toward the left shoulder. Then let your head sink toward the chest with your chin and breathe out audibly at the same time. Now stretch your head from the back of the neck, growing out of the cervical spine until it "floats" lightly and freely in the center.

This natural posture requires only a small amount of muscle strength – now you are in *balance*.

Now, you would be able to carry loads with a shoulder bar, as is the custom in China. Could you, however, carry a filled pot on your head, as women do all over Africa? If not, you have not yet achieved complete balance and will have to concentrate on centering your head.

Exercise 8:
Centring the Head

(A special exercise devised by Eva)

In order to ease tight muscles in the neck and shoulders, let your right ear sink

As a beginner, you will tend to lose your natural balance at the slightest "equine enemy action" and will therefore continuously be occupied with straightening your spine and centring your head. This is an intermediate state, however, which will not last forever.

Try *breathing* in a calm and relaxed manner in any situation, however dangerous it may seem. This calmness will transfer automatically to your equally frightened horse and will in time change a nervous wreck to a responsive riding partner. If, however, you hold your breath, your entire body will tense up, and that will confirm the horse's assumption that something incredibly dangerous is approaching!

7

The secret of light hands

The horse not only moves its body during each pace but – to the suffering of some riders – also its head, namely, in more or less pronounced nodding movements. At the trot, the movement is less pronounced; at the walk it is far more pronounced; and at the canter the very clear nodding movements are visible.

If we ramble along on a hack on a reliable horse, we let the horse walk with a slack rein. We give our horse the same chance to stretch itself with pleasure at the end and during a riding lesson. During intensive riding, on the other hand, we will need a direct contact with the horse's mouth. In order to ensure that our horse will not feel this constant contact as too disruptive, we need to keep it light, flexible, elastic and applied with the same strength at all times. For the rider, our way to achieve this would

be to react with lightning speed, moving the arms in time with all the horse's nodding movements at all times – an unreasonable requirement!

We should, therefore, use the "self-service shop" method. Offer the horse a relaxed arm, including all groups of muscles surrounding the arm. This way, it can nod at its own convenience.

The shoulder joint is a ball-and-socket joint, with the muscles, tendons, and ligaments arranged around the ball of the joint in a star formation. The required relaxing process needs to begin here, at the attachment area of all muscle groups. This relaxing process is of particular importance in moments of perceived danger.

In such a situation, if we tense up in the neck and shoulder area, we are unable to offer the horse a relaxed arm and thereby a

Exercise 9a: Overall relaxing process of the shoulder joint.

hang loosely at your sides. Imagine that a large clock is mounted on the side of your upper arm. Now start relaxing the attachment area of your upper arm clockwise. Circle backwards in slow and, to begin with, large, rotational movements. Consciously work muscle cord by muscle cord "around the clock." Later the swinging circles become smaller and smaller and are eventually practically invisible. In its refined form, this exercise is in fact more a form of "mental" swinging, but it relaxes all the same.

Eva likes working with the image that a ball circles in the joint. Maybe, you prefer this version yourself.

Your pectoral muscles could be slightly shortened due to the constant slipping of the thoracic girdle to the front. In this case, you don't just have to relax, but should also try to expand the muscles.

light contact with the reins. Therefore, we should try to perform this conscious relaxation process.

Exercise 9a:
Overall Relaxing Process
of the Shoulder Joint

On the ball or a chair, straighten your spine correctly – thoracic girdle and head in balance – and let your arms

These relaxing swinging circles will also give you a feeling of well-being, after sitting in front of the computer for hours – and I know what I am talking about! The strained discs of the cervical vertebrae area and the constantly overstretched area of the neck and shoulders often lead to head- and backaches. These relaxing swinging motions are an effective remedy.

The term "hands," repeatedly used in riding, is really more a symbolic way of say-

Slumped, rounded shoulders, and in addition to that, heavy hands. This position restricts any supple forward nodding motion of the horse's head and in the end blocks all motion of the horse.

It gets worse – inflexible hands in combination with "looking down on the horse" and therefore more weight on the horse's forelegs.

Stiff on one side: no more brutal hands, but still not quite what we want. The inside hand demonstrates some sensitivity, but the outer hand still tends to stiffen up.

ing it. In reality, it refers to the entire arm – which can admittedly be a bit confusing.

The seemingly light and elegant posture of the hands and arms of an experienced rider – the famous light hand – will be a far more wobbly affair in the case of the novice rider. Problems of balance not only lead to unsteady hands; the head wobbles, and the legs move hither and thither. In this situation, however, it would be completely wrong to want to keep the hands still. Only a statue can achieve this, as there can be no immobility in a movement! The visually apparent stillness of the hands can only be achieved by following this movement, that of the circling of the shoulders. Keeping the swinging motion in rhythm with the movement of the horse, however, must never terminate at the shoulder joint.

Exercise 9b: Overall relaxing process of the elbow joint allowing the movement to pass through the wrist.

Exercise 9b:
Overall Relaxing Process
of the Elbow Joint

On the ball or a chair: Let the swinging movement that originates in the shoulder swing through the elbow joint – naturally by means of a considerably smaller, weaker momentum. Here, you will no longer have to be active – simply let it happen.

Allowing the Movement to Pass Through the Wrist

Now the movement begins to slowly lessen, to ebb away. Allow this to happen by consciously holding your wrists relaxed enough that the swinging momentum can flow though to the relaxed fingers.

No horse is ever born with a mouth of iron. This is always the result of a rider with tight shoulder muscles and a heavy hand. The better a horse has been ridden, the lighter will be the contact that it looks for. In other words, it is not the rider who is establishing this contact, but the horse.

There will of course be situations in which we consciously have to maintain a stronger contact with the horse's mouth to push the horse (or hindquarters) forward. These short corrective moments must always be carried out while the rider rides the horse forwards intensively and never from a rigid, fixated shoulder.

Walk: During the walk, the calmest pace, everybody feels well. Most riders don't yet know how difficult it actually is to ride a horse on the bit correctly. The slow pace can lead to the rider losing the feeling of the tempo; in other words, he stops relaxing his shoulder joints, forgets elbows and wrists completely, and thus comes to a stop in the reins. This leads to faults that are difficult to correct, for example, the horse walking laterally – both legs on each side move together, like a camel. Once a horse has developed this wrong gait, it will always return to it. Therefore, a novice rider should ride as little as possible at the walk on the bit.

Far better to include rest periods at the walk on a loose rein – this ensures that no faults develop.

Don't forget to let the horse have rests during the schooling session!
The horse should relax itself and stretch its head forward and downward.

Trot: Rarely is a beginner able to relax correctly and in rhythm at a fast trot – this would definitely be asking too much of him. Simply consciously relaxing the shoulders in a circular motion, circling the elbow joints and relaxing the wrist is quite enough in the beginning.

With time, the rider will slowly begin to learn the precise rhythm of the trot. As an adult, however, you must always take into account that each disturbance or insecurity at the fast pace of the trot will *immediately* lead to a blockage of all these joints.

We are unable to prevent this reflex, but we will have to learn to react automatically: if anything scares you or makes you feel insecure, you **immediately** need to relax your shoulder, elbow, and wrist.

Canter: This pace most distinctly lifts us up from the horse. Therefore the circular relaxation of the shoulder joints and the circulation and relaxation in the elbows and wrists need to be carried out particularly well.

Every upward motion of the horse leads to an automatic tightening of the muscles of the rider. The more experienced you become, the faster you will be able to react to it, and finally relax automatically.

In the end you will even be able to start to relax and let your shoulders sink lower during the upward motion.

8

Emergency schooling aids

In most cases, this term defines the artificial schooling aids riders use when they have reached the limit of their knowledge. It doesn't matter which additional artificial schooling aid is used, in every case the head is pulled down mechanically, in other words, with force, in order to prevent the horse from evading the rider's aids by hollowing its back. Any kind of pressure, however, creates a counter-pressure, in other words, resistance. Even if the majority of modern schooling aids only start applying pressure when the horse tosses up its head, they still represent an interference with the horse's freedom of movement.

Especially when working with a schooling aid, the fast cure of the horse trainer is often mistaken for the riding attempts of the novice rider. If a horse owner has frustrated his mount with a cramped, clinging seat and

heavy hands to such an extent that it hollows its back from the moment it sees the saddle, the horse needs an expert rider to re-school it. People expect miracles from him. For this reason alone the expert, with little time on his hands, has to use the schooling rein to bring down the horse's head for a start and then to calm and relax the horse with a gentle seat and light hands so that it finally yields and allows the expert to ride it properly.

When a horse jumps, its back is rounded upward particularly high and the muscles need to stretch extensively, especially when jumping high fences. In the same way that gymnasts warm up before a competition and do stretching exercises, some show-jumping riders swear by similar stretching exercises, bringing the horse's head down with the aid of an additional schooling rein. Usually, the preferred option is the draw reins. Whether in the hands of an experienced rider doing dressage or of a show-jumping expert warming up his horse in a particular way, the schooling rein can be used if the exercise has a purpose and as long as the rider's hands do not become heavy and rigid.

A schooling rein can also be practical as a support for a novice rider. In those riding schools with an indoor arena, the evenings are often the busiest time. Lungeing lessons require time and personnel, however, so novices are often sent in groups into the large area of the riding arena or in some cases are not lunged at all. In order to protect the horse from the inept hands of the novice, the horse can be ridden with side reins, with the De Gouge, the Harbridge training aid, the Equi-lunge, or the famous "elastic training aid," which all produce a connection between the horse's head and its mouth and the saddle girth. This enables the novice rider to concentrate more on his seat in the first lessons off the lunge rein, and the horse will be handled less severely in its mouth. This situation justifies the use of a schooling rein, even if a weak rider tries his best on a slightly spoiled horse, but has not

yet acquired the skill of being able to ride the horse forwards with a relaxed back and momentum without the support of the schooling aid.

It is a completely different affair, however, if the rider constantly uses schooling reins. These riders generally prefer the draw reins, never having understood that this dangerous schooling aid should only be applied during the short moment of correction. Once the horse has given up its resistance, it should immediately be ridden only on the snaffle bit.

In order to be able to correct a horse with the help of draw reins, the rider not only needs to have a very light hand that reacts instantly – in other words, able to swing perfectly in the shoulder joint – but also needs to ride forwards very efficiently at the moment of correction. In short, draw reins are best left to skilled and sensitive riders.

The horse indicates each seat or hand error on the part of the rider, not only through its movement, but also through the posture of its head. A completely "tied-up" horse does not have the freedom to signal these errors.

Therefore, many unbearably self-assured "super riders" shamble along for years on their initially very good and often very

The use of the drawing reins from a medical point of view. The continuous use of the drawing reins leads to tension of the upper muscles of the horse's spine and to an increased strain on the poll area and the thoracic vertebrae. It thereby blocks the thoracic and lumbar vertebrae, prevents the relaxed and swinging back of the horse, causes pain and medical damage, and is not only counterproductive, but also poses a threat to animal welfare. – Veterinary surgeon Andrea Prikler

expensive prize horses. The head position of the horse can no longer betray its rider – so they believe – but you will wait in vain if you expect flowing paces and swinging momentum. These horses, which are tied down and often ridden with bits as sharp as knives, can almost bite their chest. The unmistakable indicators of these weak but overbearing riders are fixed shoulder joints, fists of iron, and repeated use of the draw

reins. In addition, these riders then alternately pull the left and right rein (known as sawing the mouth with the reins) – they learned this from watching some third-rate show jumper, and they believe that this form of riding is the classy thing.

Have a look around an indoor or outdoor riding school. How many schooling aids can you see, and which of them are emergency schooling aids?

9

How does a horse move?

Although a horse has four legs, they do not all perform the same function. The straight forelegs have the predominant function of carrying the weight, while the angled hind legs create the forward and upward thrust.

Therefore, people say that the engine of the horse lies in the hindquarters. Muscle chains ensure that the momentum that is developed in the hindquarters is transferred via the rounded back to the forehand.

The muscles of the horse are all directly connected from the head to the hindquarters.

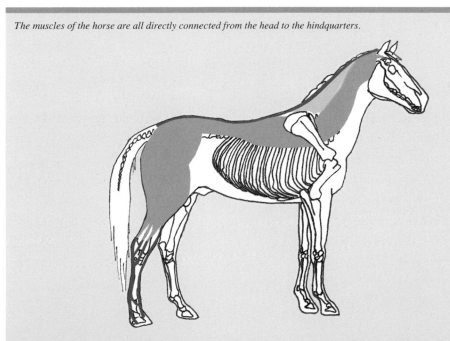

Even a foal will produce elegant motions. Blockages are only built up by an incorrectly seated rider.

Depending on the pace, either side of the horse's back is lifted up or lowered down, as the respective muscle cord that runs along the spine tightens or relaxes. During this intensive muscle activity, the horse's back would prefer to be free and undisturbed.

Unfortunately, however, there is a rider on top! Depending on his ability, he will disturb the horse to a greater or lesser degree.

The muscles of the hindquarters, the back

muscles, and the nuchal ligament right up to the mouth are all connected in one long flow. This direct connection enables us to control a horse weighing over half a ton with a minimum of effort.

If we disturb this sensitive connection by means of a heavy passive seat or hard clinging thighs, a hard-working, friendly horse will turn into a bad-tempered one, maybe quite suddenly becoming an exploding bundle of resistance. It is not only the strong

Elegance and flexibility of the horse in carriage driving can be achieved by riding the driving horses correctly. Odette is ridden intermediate dressage on a regular basis.

back muscles of the horse that move in rhythm. Their counterparts, the muscles of the abdomen, collaborate in the same rhythm. When a hind hoof swings forward, the muscles of the horse's abdomen also move. We don't just feel the lifting and lowering movements under our buttocks, our legs also feel a constant in and out of the abdomen. Therefore, we have to give room not only to the back muscles, but also to those of the abdomen. After all, our hor-

se is a living creature which wants to be able to breathe freely and unimpeded – clinging riders' legs are definitely a hindrance here.

The active hindquarters alone via the arched back are unable to build up sufficient momentum and tension in the horse to keep it under control pleasantly and, at the same time, reasonably secure without resorting to force. This control can only come from our seat bones and buttocks and our legs. The hands are of practically no account – something that the novice rider will find almost impossible to believe.

At a faster pace, the entire topline of the horse becomes flatter, and the pressure on the reins automatically becomes slightly heavier. The extreme form can be observed in racehorses. In the collected paces, on the other hand, the neck, back, and croup show a rounded arched shape. The hindquarters no longer just push the horse forward, they now also carry more weight and relieve the weight on the forehand. This means that the horse itself only looks for a light contact with the reins.

Somebody renting a horse for a lesson will not only expect that the horse is fit, but also hopes that it is well behaved and willing to execute the rider's every command as fast as lightning. However, any horse can only move as well as its conformation and its state of health allow, how the saddle and bridle fit, and, first and foremost, to what degree the rider allows it to perform its duties.

Horses are not machines. Although they are normally very friendly and in most cases quite willing to obey, they also have bad and good days. If horses could talk, riding school horses would probably talk incessantly about their illnesses and injuries – it's no wonder that they are often in a bad mood.

They are the heavy workers in this sport and receive little thanks.

10

Swinging hips – let's move!

We now come to the actual riding movements of the pelvis, the constant *swinging in harmony* with the movement of the horse. This comprises two totally different motions that fuse into one process of movement:

• the overall relaxation of the hip joints
• the pelvis swing.

Generally, only children and adolescents can comprehend this combination of movements. Learning to ride as an adult involves constant checking to see whether one is neglecting any part of the movement. Sometimes, if the situation requires it, we will employ one part with extra force, for example, swinging the pelvis to drive the horse forward.

The riding school teacher is of little help in correcting the movement of swinging in harmony, as he is unable, in some cases, to recognize the small blockages that the rider has put in place when he neglects one part of the movement. The only thing the teacher can observe is that the horse has stopped swinging its back in a relaxed manner. It either stops going forward with impetus, runs off, or shows its displeasure in some other way.

The hip joint – like the shoulder joint – is a ball-and-socket joint. However, it is much larger and stronger and, as in the case of the shoulder, is encircled by muscles, tendons, and ligaments in a star formation. In order to ride well, we need not only a light hand, but also very soft buttocks and supple legs. This can only be achieved through constant relaxation of the hip joint.

The overall relaxing process has been shown to work extremely well with the shoulder joint. Therefore, we will use this method in the same way for the hip joints.

Exercise 10a: Overall relaxing process of the hip joints.

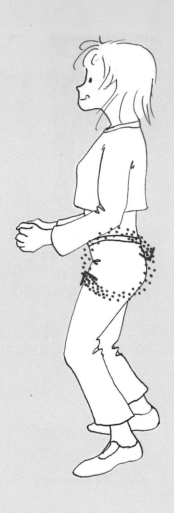

In the beginning, we will require a bit more freedom of movement, so we will first practise this exercise standing up, then sitting down. The physio-ball is an excellent object to carry out this exercise, much better than a chair.

Exercise 10a:
Overall Relaxing Process of the Hip Joint – Standing Up

Stand with your legs slightly apart with very relaxed knees. This posture is similar to that of a sailor in a storm. Maintain the correct upright position of your vertebrae, with the thoracic girdle and the head in balance.

Once more, imagine that you are wearing a large clock. This time, it is mounted on the side of your hip.

Visualize the attachment area of your thigh, and start relaxing your hip joint in backward rotational movement. Consciously work, muscle cord by muscle cord, "around the clock."

This swinging relaxation is identical with the rotation in the shoulder joint. The only thing that makes this exercise more difficult in the hip joint is that there are considerably more tense muscles. After all, our hip joint is our largest and strongest joint.

On the ball: Sit down on the ball in the correct upright position – thoracic girdle and head in balance – and practise the relaxing swinging movements of the pelvis as described above. If you have already become used to this exercise, then practise it unilaterally. You will find that if you are right-handed, you will probably be significantly less skilled with your left hip. Compensate for this through increased exercises on this side. Try working with the image that a ball is circling in the joint.

Swinging in harmony with the horse's movement takes place primarily in the hip joints. From here, the movement moves down to the relaxed knees, the loose ankles, and the heels and balls of the feet, which absorb the motion in the stirrup iron. All these joints can only work in harmony if the rhythm in the hip joints is not pinched, clamped, and throttled. As with the steady hands, the desired, seemingly steady leg is only a sequence of the relaxed swinging motion, the movement in harmony with the horse. If, on the other hand, the knees are fixed rigidly, the rider's legs are pressed against the horse's sides in convulsion, the heels of the feet are pulled up or pushed down grimly, then we cannot speak of a steady leg but instead only of a rigid "dead" leg, with which no one can ride.

Exercise 10b:
Overall Relaxing Process
of the Hip Joint Standing Up

Let the swinging movement that originates in the hip joints swing through the knee joints – naturally, by means of a considerably smaller, weaker momentum. You will no longer have to be active – simply let it happen.

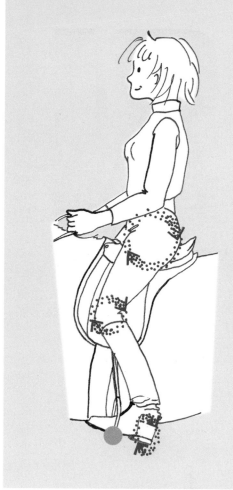

Exercise 10b: Swinging relaxation of the knee joint, swinging relaxation and flexion of the ankle, flexion of the ball of the foot.

Overall Relaxing Process and Absorption of the Movement by the Ankle

The movement already begins to fade away; the heels sink rhythmically with the remnants of the movement. Finally,

Swinging in harmony with the horse's movement can feel completely different, depending on the conformation of the horse. Temptation is a large horse with a relatively short, strained back – very difficult to ride.

the Absorption of the Movement by the Ball of the Foot in the Stirrup

Naturally, it is impossible actually to practice the absorption of the movement sitting on the physio-ball. However, it is sufficient to feel this movement pass through these joints, rather than keeping the joints stiff and rigid.

The fast rhythm of the horse and the powerful basic movements constitute an enormous strain for the novice rider. This continuous boring loosening-up program, which now needs to be executed constantly on the horse, naturally tends to get mixed up again and again, and it isn't much fun either. Riding should be fun! It will be in the future, but only if we fight our way through this decisive loosening-up phase and don't simply push it aside.

No adult novice rider – and that includes all those adolescents after they have been through puberty – is able to completely switch off this aggravating automatic tightening up of the hip joints.

Jantar the young colt has not yet achieved balance and requires a very flexible rider who can swing in motion and who has no problems with her feeling of balance.

Therefore, at the beginning of his riding career the novice rider will very consciously and actively have to loosen up rhythmically during practically every movement of the horse. Only with time will the automatic tightening up be replaced by the automatic pleasurable relaxation.

It does not help when you realize that there is no time to enjoy riding in the beginning because you are constantly employed in outwitting the closing and clutching reflexes of your legs. It is even more frustrating when you believe you have discovered that

children and adolescents, i.e., young adults who have been riding constantly since their childhood, don't seem to have this problem. This impression, however, is an illusion. Have a closer look at the riders in the riding arena! How many loose, harmoniously swinging thighs, how many relaxed knees, how many gently flexing heels do you see, and how many more or less clinging thighs with blocked pelvises can you recognize? How many rigid, tight youthful shoulders can you count? Why do so-called advanced riders always go back to riding without stirrups? Why do the so-called advanced riders also ride with wobbly heads? The truth is and will always be: all advanced riders also drag around with them their urge to cling on – only very skillful children and profes-sional riders who spend their lives in the saddle are likely not to be haunted by this phenomenon.

Don't let yourself become insecure, and don't give up! The most important thing you need is a suitable, calm horse that you can trust and on which you can relax completely. Leave joyfully bucking horses to young riders. Of course, at some point you will fall off; if you learn to ride, this is part and parcel, but don't overdo it. At the moment you are lacking the necessary skill to be able to ride more difficult horses safely.

Don't keep only to the riding arena, but start hacking out as soon as you have learned the necessary basic know-how. To begin with, ride in company with an experienced rider on a calm horse.

Important: you can chat, but still constantly need to carry out your loosening-up programme – at every pace.

Initially avoid hacks with a large number of riders. This will only upset your horse unnecessarily, and you will tense up instead of relaxing. To begin with, favour the walk with long reins, but hold on to the pommel of the saddle for added safety. And remember that the countryside can be full of unexpected hazards, including rabbits and pheasants. Even the most obedient horse in the world can take fright and suddenly jump aside if one of these fellow creatures suddenly jumps out in front of it, or even if a motorcycle backfires.

Something's happening down below

Horses with little movement in their backs are rare. Normally, we need more communication options than just the loosening up of the pelvis and hip joints, not only for swinging in harmony, but also in particular when we ask the horse to perform a task. We will now start additionally communicating with the horse with the help of the muscles of the lower abdomen – we become belly dancers.

The pelvis is connected firmly with the spine. However, it is able to rock backwards and forwards like a swing. The muscles of the abdomen control this swinging motion. We have to use the lowest part of the abdomen when riding. Even if you are a fairly athletic person, you will probably hardly ever use these muscles.

The most important task for the abdominal wall is that of holding and protecting the intestines. For this reason – probably – the straight muscles of the abdomen are separated into horizontal subsections of approximately 5 centimetres.

The most often executed gymnastic exercises usually only exercise the upper part of the abdomen; the lowest segment is hardly ever used. However, it is precisely this part we need, as we can tilt the pelvis with the help of these muscles and thus follow the rhythm of the movement of the horse. This means that we have to exercise this part of the abdomen!

We will predominantly use the angular abdominal muscles, which we use daily when rotating the upper body, for riding turns and circles.

In ismacogy, the upward and downward swinging motion of the pelvis is called the pelvic swing.

The difficulty with this exercise is that we cannot "start off" the lowest area of the abdomen. However, the following exercise might allow us to do it after all.

Exercise 11:
Pelvic Swing

Standing up: Adopt the sailor's posture again, in other words, a slight straddling position and extremely relaxed knees. Remain in a correct upright position of the spine, with the thoracic girdle and head in balance.

Imagine that you want to close the zip of a pair of trousers. Unfortunately, the zip is stuck right at the bottom. What can you do now? You will now involuntarily tense up the lowest part of your abdomen and thereby also tilt the pelvis, in order to free the zip. After that, relax the abdomen, and the pelvis will swing back into its original position.

If you stand with your back against a wall and practise the pelvic swing there, you will feel distinctly how the spine straightens up through the tilting of the pelvis.

Lying down: You can also take up the battle with the zip by lying down on your back, with legs slightly apart and knees lifted off the ground. Make sure that only the pelvis swings and that the spine stays in close contact with the ground. Push your hands under your buttocks, and check whether your buttocks also remain relaxed during the exercise.

On the physio-ball: Sit on the ball in a correct upright posture – the thoracic girdle and head in balance – and take up the battle with the zip as described above.

If you have become fairly adept at executing the exercise, practise it unilaterally. You will discover again that you have a skilful and a less skilful side.

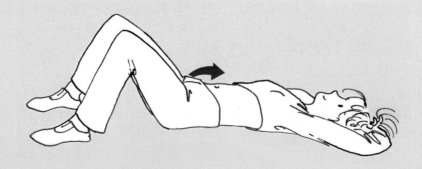

Exercise 11: Pelvic swing lying on the back.

*Solitaire, the perfectly trained older mare, has good conformation and offers the rider an extremely pleasant motion
– the ideal beginner's horse.*

The term "swing" can be misleading, because you automatically think of a regular swinging motion forward and backward. However, you should only swing upward in the front and then return to your original position.

If you swing back, you will end up in the unhealthy terminal posture of each vertebra: the hollow back.

The pelvic swing is also considered to be particularly healthy in ismacogy. Through the massage-like pumping motions, the spine becomes incredibly activated. The intestines are also mobilized and any digestive problems will become less acute. The back muscles, the supporting corset for the spine, are strengthened, and the tensions that develop after hours of one-sided work will disappear.

Now we come to *swinging in harmony* with the movement of the horse. The combination is as follows.

Billy the Haflinger is fairly high on his hind end and can only be ridden with a light hand contact via the back, if the rider is in good balance and can swing with the motion.

Exercise 12: Overall loosening up of the hip joints and pelvic swing.

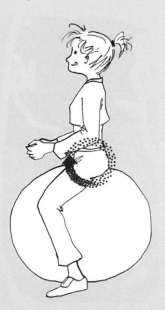

Exercise 12:
Overall Loosening Up
of the Hip Joints and Pelvic Swing

Standing up: Adopt the sailor's posture again, in other words, a slight straddling position and extremely relaxed knees. Remain in a correct upright position of the spine, with the thoracic girdle and head in balance.

If you combine the rotating overall loosening up of the hip joints with the pelvic swing in the same rhythm, this will result in even *swinging circles* – the riding movement which we adopt on

In the case of New Jack City the Quarter horse stallion, the movements are smaller due to its breed. Therefore, it is much easier for the rider to swing with the motion.

straight lines, if we are not asking the horse to do anything special.

On the ball: Here the swinging circles can be practiced so perfectly that you will almost feel that you are sitting on a horse. It is important that you keep up executing everything we have learned so far and don't suddenly start tightening up somewhere.

Keep on checking yourself by pushing your hands under your buttocks during the swinging exercise.

Now you can also start practising the exercise unilaterally, as you will be swinging unilaterally in all paces.

Each horse will react very positively to these swinging circles, will become calm and relaxed, and will start walking with its back arched correctly. And if the rider uses a bit too much momentum by mistake, the horse won't react with bad temper.

We will also use the swinging motions and turns in all other riding movements. The type of turn, however, will change a bit; for example, when riding a curved line, the circle will become an ellipse.

Riding and dancing have a lot in common. The closer the body contact is in combined movements, the more the movements should be executed in harmony. If one partner doesn't know the dancing steps, dancing will become a misery for the other. Both partners needs to know and feel what is going to happen in order to achieve harmony. If one partner always makes the respective movements too late, this hinders the other and prevents the creation of harmony.

The same applies to riding. The rider needs to know and feel exactly the back movements of his horse at each pace. Only this will allow him to anticipate the horse's movement.

To begin with, we will only deal with the two paces, walk and trot. We leave the canter to a later time on purpose, as we will need a type of rotating feeling for the canter that we will have to learn first.

Exercise 13:
Paces

On the physio-ball: Straighten your spine correctly – thoracic girdle and head in balance – and combine the rotating overall loosening up of the hip joints with the pelvic swing to achieve the swinging circles, as described above.

The **walk** is a four-time striding pace. Both feet of each side lift one after the other: the left hind leg, the left foreleg, then the right hind leg and the right foreleg.
Therefore, practise as follows: twice on one side, twice on the other, in slow sequence.

At the **trot**, the diagonal pairs of legs move simultaneously, in other words, the front left and the right hind, then the front right and left hind.
Therefore, practise once left and once right in fairly quick succession.

Light seat bones and muscles

Even Xenophon had difficulty in describing the rider's seat on a horse. He finally came up with the definition: "A type of standing with bent legs."

When a person sits down he places himself on his seat bones, also known as seat cartilage. This is a sleigh-like construction where the runners are wide and broad at the back and come together at a raised and acute angle at the front where they form the pubis. An essential difference to the sleigh is that our runners, or rockers, do not have straight undersides, but are instead slightly rounded all the way. When we are in an upright chair we tilt forwards and backwards on these runners all the time. At the same time, we keep our upper body in balance with the help of muscles. In order to facilitate this, it helps to have an additional support, the back of the chair.

On a horse we can forget about any seating support: no chair back, no immovable seat, and to top it all, only a very small supporting surface. An explanation of why this seat is so very small can be derived from a mathematical principle: "If two curves touch, their area of contact is reduced to a point."

In the event that the horse has already been warmed up and is walking forwards with impulsion with a correctly arched back, this means that the slightly rounded rockers of the person and the arched spine of the horse come into contact. Thus – to a degree – the area of contact forms a point.

It is precisely this point that we have to find and feel. It will become the essence of your riding ability!

A saddle deceives us visually. It might appear to offer a broad seat surface, but that

The following should not really be seen as an exercise which can be practiced, but do try out Exercise 14 at some point. You will be surprised at what you feel.

Exercise 14:
Getting a Feel for the Seat Bones

On the chair: We now need – however comical that may sound – a rolling pin, which should be present in almost every household.

This round wooden appliance has an approximate diameter of 10 centimetres and is around 50 centimetres long, and is used for rolling out pastry. Place it on the hardest chair you can find. Then sit down on it.

The difference to before is that we are now sitting on a deliberately reduced seat surface. The muscles of the buttocks can only cushion little, we distinctly feel our seat bones. The horse feels these as distinctly as we do!

Exercise 14: Get a feel for the seat bones.

is simply not the case. An English saddle is barely able to protect the horse, because the contact area can only be increased to a small extent, and our seat bones are dangerously near to the back of the horse.

The smaller the supporting surface, the higher the pressure that develops on these few square centimetres.

A good rider changes this weight pressure into a forward-swinging motion.

A bad rider allows his weight to fall heavily and with a thud onto the horse's back, and bores his seat bones into the horse's back.

Rider with too long stirrup leathers,
sitting precariously and unbalanced.

Rider with her stirrups too short,
forcing her into a crouched sitting position.

That explains why a delicate horse can often look pretty pleased with a well-nourished rider, whereas a large, strong horse ridden by a feather-light rider tightens its back muscles and looks unhappy. These two different types of seat, which can be seen everywhere, demonstrate how difficult it is on a horse to always find the ideal central position on our rockers. If the rider rolls too far forward on his rockers, he is **sitting**

The correct seat.

If the rider rolls too far backward on his rockers, he collapses in the lower back – but not on the loins of the horse; that is determined by the position of the saddle rather than the rider. This not only strains the sensitive area of the horse's kidneys, but the rider will also adopt for himself a very insecure posture, with no control over the horse.

The saddle is, of course, of the greatest importance for the rider's seat. Not only does it need to fit the horse, in other words, it must not impair the freedom of movement of the horse's back and shoulders, but it should also allow the rider to adopt the ideal central position.

Through their high build up and the long panels, the military saddles of long ago, which had to fit any horse and rider, alleviated the possible pressure on the horse's back and, in particular, protected the spine. Modern Western saddles still do this to a certain degree.

The bad rider will not be experienced as particularly painful. However, the good rider cannot develop a light contact with the horse's back in such a saddle. If I sit on a normal English saddle, my seat bones can cause considerable damage, which means that I need to keep them under constant control – that is the meaning of *light seat bones and muscles*. It is the constant attempt to make sure not to press down on the horse, with a thud, heavily and immobile, but instead to swing forwards with momentum and lightness.

on his pubic bone rather than his seat bone. Instead of sitting on the buttocks, the rider sits on his upper legs and strains the already overstrained forehand of the horse.

A very common fault: too short stirrup leathers which push the rider's buttocks back, her legs in front of the vertical, as well as hunched shoulders.

Unbalanced seat with too long stirrups.

"If it weren't a luxury ..."

"If it weren't a luxury, each horse that has a natural talent for using its back muscles, a natural and swinging pace could, in our opinion, be schooled by a good rider by exclusively employing the seat aids, and learn to be ridden in collection."

This statement from Otto de la Croix shows us that a skilled seat can obviously do far more than simply swing in relaxed motion, in harmony with the horse's movements. One of the basic precepts of the "Haute École," the classical art of riding is: Ride your horse **forward!** If every lesson can, in principle, be achieved purely by seat aids, this clear marching command needs to originate in the seat.

Forward is a request which s not linked to a specific pace. It is solely addressed to the hind legs of the horse and requires the legs to step forwards energetically with lon-

ger stride and in a certain sense also carry the rider's weight. A horse will not offer this increased gymnastic effort by itself. Therefore, a rider who simply swings with the motion of the horse, without using his seat is "away with the fairies." To make sure that we do not make the same mistake, we will instead learn to ride forward.

Exercise 15:
Riding Forward from the Seat

Standing and on the physio-ball: Arrange yourself in a correct upright posture, with the thoracic girdle and head in balance.
Swing at the walk or the trot. Now mentally increase these circles and strengthen the pelvic swing.

At the same time, emphasize the lower part of the forward swinging motion by means of a distinct impulse.

Exercise 15: Riding forward from the seat.

If you can manage to keep all the muscles of the buttocks and thighs relaxed, a sensitive, well-trained horse will react to this command. The technical term for this is the rather confusing "bracing of the back." The rider's back muscles are active as counter-partners of the muscles of the abdomen, but in reality, it is the particularly active pelvic swing, in other words, the muscles of the abdomen, that induce the forwards motion; therefore, this term of command is potentially rather misleading.

Every time a rider fails to perform a movement, he attempts to achieve his target anyway by carrying out substitute actions. The term "back" simply tempts the rider to tense up a part of the rear of his body. The most commonly tightened up are the muscles of the buttocks (seat) and the muscle groups which run along the back of the thighs.

If the command is "Push forward with your back," the misunderstanding with the back is joined by the attempt to use force.

There is only a hair's breadth between force and weight, and the rider will immediately push his seat bones into the horse's back and will wonder why the horse is now refusing to cooperate at all.

Since not all horses are highly sensitive, however, we also like to use another type of aid to move forward: the leg aids.

"Put into simple terms, the leg aids are never main aids, but should only ever be

seen as supporting aids. You need to move forwards by adopting the correct seat, adjusting and subjugating yourself to it, and use the legs with the awareness that, on their own, they are practically worthless without the correct utilization of the seat."

The truth of de la Croix's statement can be observed in every riding arena. Not just novice riders, but also the so-called advanced riders belabour the sides of their horses with their heels in the most unappealing way – pushing and kicking, they attempt to force the forward motion. Despite this, or probably because of it, they achieve no real success, as this kicking makes the horses drag along with a particular lack of enthusiasm.

The hip joint can turn our entire leg outward, while the knee joint is more responsible for the lower thigh. Special muscles which create a connection between the pelvis and the knee – Schusdziarra calls them riding muscles – allow us to bypass the thighs by applying a small rotation to the outside, a small motion of the knee and hip joint, in order to turn the calf to lie against the horse's sides.

If we now bend the knee slightly with the help of these muscles and tighten the calf muscle, which runs along the back side of the lower thigh, by letting the heel of the foot sink down, we have a perfect forward driving leg.

How can we accustom ourselves to this slight outward rotation, which cannot in any way be a gymnastic exercise? Let us try using the ismacogy again.

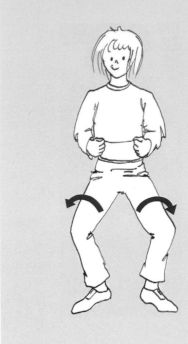

Exercise 16: Turning of columns.

Exercise 16:
Turning of Columns

Initially standing up, then on the physio-ball: Stand with slightly straddled legs and relaxed knees. Imagine your feet are columns that you want to turn slightly outwards from the inside. However, "shift" only the skin and a certain amount of muscle, but do not turn the knees outward.

Once we have become accustomed to the slight rotating feel, we combine the forward driving seat with the driving thighs. Only this lower thigh coming from behind is a real aid moving along the horse's side in a massaging motion as if it wanted to move the horse's side along with it in a slight turning motion.

The foot, which is pushed outward and thumps the horse's side, only causes the horse pain, producing a reluctance to co-operate.

Exercise 17:
Riding Forward with the Seat and Calves

Standing up and on the physio-ball: In a correct upright posture, the thoracic girdle and head in balance, swing either at the walk or trot.
Mentally enlarge these circles and strengthen the pelvic swing. At the same time, emphasize the lower part of the forward swinging motion by means of a distinct impulse. Every time the horse lowers its back, in other words, begins to swing its hind leg forward, and you give a distinct forward impulse in the lower part of the swinging circle, you also rotate the briefly tightened calf against the horse.
Afterwards relax the calf again immediately.
This rhythm is repeated with every swinging circle.

Exercise 17: Riding forward with the seat and calves.

Sometimes one command to move forward is sufficient. If, on the other hand, my horse has decided to have a relaxed day, I will have to drive it forward a few times – after all, we aren't always so keen to have to work either.

If I only smack my thighs against the horse's sides, it will tense up and will move with its head thrown up high, an evasive back, and tight strides. A horse which is ridden in this manner without the seat is technically said to be a horse that goes against the leg.

This kind of riding will inevitably lead to back problems for the rider as well as for the horse.

If you have it, flaunt it! Longer rider's legs can push forwards the hindquarters of the horse far easier than if the rider's legs are short.

Trust is a great thing; control is better. Even if you believe that you are remaining relaxed when riding forwards, that may not be the case at all. Place your hands palms upwards under your buttocks and check whether you are really not tightening any muscles – neither in the back part of the thighs nor in your buttocks. You should only feel a round swinging motion. It is extremely strenuous to perform this exercise in a completely relaxed and at the same time correct manner. Therefore, make sure that you take plenty of rest periods, because, of course, you will not be driving the horse constantly!

Control

From a mechanical point of view, each horse is fitted with rear-wheel drive. With our seat, we not only determine the "engine power" but also the direction in which our horse is expected to go. The forehand of the horse is pushed by the hindquarters, just like the front wheels of a car with rear-wheel drive.

To steer in straight lines looks simple. We are sitting straight and believe that our horse will now move forwards in a straight line. It cannot do this, however, as it has a certain natural bend to one side, just like a dog. The forehand of a horse is usually narrower than its hindquarters. Therefore, a horse not only moves with a slight bend but is also more resistant on the other side. It usually places its right hind leg slightly outward. This bend to one side cannot be corrected via the reins but only through the seat. Riding lateral movements is the easiest way

to achieve this. As these movements are too complicated for us at this stage, we will deal with these corrections later. D'Auvergne's statement: *"The horse rider with all his perfection of the art of riding will spend his life correcting this imperfection"* tells us how often and how long we will spend our time in straightening our horse.

Great implications! At least this bend to one side will guarantee that we will never be bored when riding.

How do we actually establish contact with the horse's mouth? We take up the reins, shorter and shorter, until we feel the horse's mouth evenly touching both reins. We only offer the reins to the horse, there is nothing else we can do. If we are riding forwards with a correct seat and our horse moves with a correctly arched back, it will soon accept this offer, and we suddenly experience a

67

Incorrect position of the rider's hands: turned in, hidden fists.
Here, the fists are pressed down too far.

Still incorrect: the fists are bunched up; the wrist is tensed.

The correct position for the rider's hands.

distinct flexible connection. This does not happen immediately, however. As long as the horse is not moving forwards in complete relaxation, we have problems not only with the seat. The connection with the reins also changes frequently. Once all groups of muscles work together, we will also achieve the ideal connection through the reins.

Even if our arms are correctly relaxed due to the loosening up of the shoulder joints, we can still hold a relaxed arm incorrectly. We will now procure a pair of reins, or rather substitute reins, and also train the correct, relaxed rein arms, to complement the correct seat.

Use the long, soft belt of a dressing gown. It would be even better to tie two

In Western riding, the reins hang loosely; the horse is expected to achieve its own balance and motion.

of these terry-cloth belts together. This ensures that the reins are long enough. The only important thing is that the material is flexible. Place your physio-ball approximately 70 centimetres behind a chair and place the substitute reins around the back of the chair, at the level of the seat of the physio-ball – this approximately corresponds to the height of the horse's head.

We can thus imitate the reins situation to a certain degree.

It would be even better, of course, if you could ask somebody to play the horse, simulating the nodding motion of the horse's head. Then the entire arm could move with every movement, and the lightest movements could also be checked with the flexible fingers.

Exercise 18:
Position of the Arms and Reins

On the physio-ball: Sit in a correct upright posture and take up the substitute reins. Let the upper arms hang down straight and relaxed. The lower arms should be held in such a way that the line from the elbow to the horse's mouth remains unbroken.

The direct shortest connection between the elbow and the horse's mouth is the ideal contact.

The elbow joint and wrist swing in time with the movement of the horse in a relaxed manner originating from the shoulder joint. The relaxed upright fist only continues the direct line from the lower arm. It should never be turned inward or outward. The thumbs rest on top of the wrist in a relaxed, slightly bent manner.

Organize a whip, or something resembling a whip, for example a wooden spoon, and hold this "whip" loosely in one hand, together with the reins.

Twisted, rigid hands can be recognized very clearly through the whip sticking out almost horizontally.

Now distinctly bounce up and down on the physio-ball and concentrate on keeping the contact with the reins even and light by overall loosening up of the shoulder joint in rhythmic cadence.

Exercise 18: Position of the arms and reins.

If we are not only sitting correctly but also holding our hands perfectly, our horse should really be satisfied.

Unfortunately, horses prefer their comfort above everything and continue to try to free themselves from the tension that is created through riding forwards. They tug lightly on the reins – if the rider does not pay attention – until it has become 50 centimetres longer again, and they can thus comfortably trail their hindquarters, rather than relieving the weight of the rider on the forehand.

Naturally, this cannot be allowed. "Pick up the reins – keep them shorter" is the frequent command which can be heard in many riding schools in such a situation. This tempts the rider to attempt to bring the horse into shape from the front to the back – instead of riding forward. Problems with balance mean that we will sometimes use the reins as a means of support. Such an error of the hands is called stuck hands.

A well-trained, sensitive horse will become irritated immediately. Or we may not have paid attention, and one rein is hanging in a loop and in the next moment our horse receives a sharp pull in its mouth – that will make it unhappy as well.

There is nothing to stop you from apologizing to your horse, if you have committed an error, and starting again.

Always remember: impulsion is the "fuel" we need for riding. Therefore, ride forward with momentum, offer the reins to the horse again and hope that the offended horse will soon accept the reins again forgivingly.

"Halt" without the reins

On a sailing boat, we use the wind as the driving force. It acts as a forwards-driving force, regardless of which direction it is blowing from. If we want to stop, we turn the boat into the wind, that is, point its bow into the oncoming wind. The driving force then becomes a resistance, which we use as a brake. When preparing to reach the jetty correctly, we need to judge matters very precisely, to avoid ramming the jetty.

The situation is similar for riding, insofar as we only know one driving force: the *impulsion*. We ride forward with tempo because this is the means by which we control our horse. If we want to come to a halt, again we can only use this impulsion. What do we do so that this impulsion suddenly acts as a brake?

Braking is possible because our horse is able to learn. When receiving a certain sig-

nal, it has learned to collect itself, in other words, place its hind legs further under its body, i.e., its own weight, to transfer its weight further back and eventually come to a halt. This will only happen, though, if the rider uses this aid which the horse has learned with absolute precision.

A person cannot stop a half-ton horse by sheer force. If the rider does something wrong, he has no other option but to pull desperately on the reins. As horses in general are good-natured animals, our rider will eventually come to a stop, but it will be just as humiliating as ramming the jetty.

On a boat, any change of direction is declared clearly and in good time. The helmsman calls "Ready about," to which the crew will respond by calling "All clear!" and then the manoeuvre commences. Every horse would dearly like to receive his

Exercise 19: Quarter-halt.

If our horse moves forward willingly and with impulsion and we only want to indicate the commencement of a new lesson, a quarter-halt should be used. In this case, the rider will regain his balance by himself.

Exercise 19: Quarter-halt

On the ball with reins: In a correct upright posture, the thoracic girdle and head in balance the feet maintain complete contact with the floor. Pick up the substitute reins, and swing either at the walk or at the trot. Now distinctly sit up a bit more and loosen up the muscles around the hip joints, especially in the lowering rear part of the impulsion.

instructions in the same clear and distinct manner. Each transition, each new move, everything should be begun with a command that a horse can understand.

Such an announcement understood by horses is called a *halt*. Nowadays, we only use the half-halt and the full-halt. In the past, however, riders worked with quarter-halts and even eighth-halts.

This made perfect sense because these days the half-halt now has to cover a very broad spectrum. Therefore, we intend to revive the term *quarter-halt*, because a clear differentiation can contribute considerably to the understanding of these movement processes.

Very well-trained, sensitive horses will react to this simple maintaining of the balance. Usually, we use the half-halt as a preparation for new lessons and transitions. For this purpose we increase impulsion through riding forwards with increased tempo. This impulsion, developed by the hind legs, runs via the croup and back muscles and further via the muscles of the neck to the horse's mouth. There, a minute signal of the hands prohibits any further forward movement.

If there is no such "stop sign," the horse will simply run away on its forehand, driven by the forward aid. In order to maintain the impulsion and to reverse it, we close our fingers slightly for a moment. Then we immediately relax them again and re-create the normal light, flexible connection with the reins. The impulsion flows back into the engaged hind legs, which now carry more of the horse's own weight, even if we repeat these half-halts.

Now our horse has improved its balance, has built up power in its hindquarters, and is "all clear" for a new lesson.

Should we close our hands at some stage at the wrong moment, our horse feels impeded. But when is the right moment?

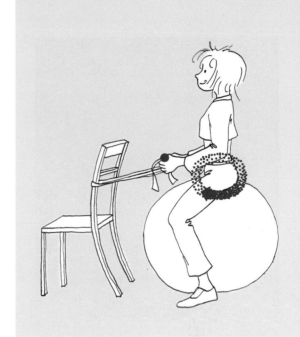
Exercise 20: Half-halt.

Exercise 20:
Half-halts

On the ball with reins: In a correct upright posture, the thoracic girdle and head in balance, the feet maintain complete contact with the floor.

Pick up the substitute rein, and swing either at the walk or at the trot. Now distinctly sit up a bit more and loosen up the muscles around the hip joints, especially in the lowering rear part of the impulsion.

Now enlarge these circles mentally and emphasize the lower part of the forward-swinging motion through an intensification of the pelvic swing by means of a distinct impulse.

This "intensified" moment, in other words, the lowest level of the swinging motion, is also the moment at which you need to close your hands for a short time, so that the impulsion is "redirected" into the engaged hindquarters. Then we immediately open them again and re-create the light flexible connection with the reins.

If necessary, you can also rotate the tight calf against the horse's side in the "intensified" moment of the swinging motion. As always, the intensity of the necessary aids is dependent on how well the horse is being ridden.

During the halt, the horse should stand squarely on all four legs, showing a good inherent posture – Donnerwetter seems to have misunderstood something somewhere along the line.

Horses are animals of flight and can be distracted very easily. If your horse isn't paying any attention, you will have to "talk" to it more often and more clearly. In other words, you will need to repeat the half-halts a few times.

All three main paces can also be ridden with *increased impulsion*. As dressage judges want to see distinctive differences to a certain degree, in order to judge the horse's ability, even novice dressage tests require the horse to be ridden at the working and medium trot, as well as at the working and medium canter. However, the increased impulsion, performed properly, is a difficult movement and should not be expected at the basic working level.

Irrespective of which pace is ridden at an extended tempo, the horse must never move its legs faster than normal.

The horse should instead lengthen its strides (lengthen its outline, as it is called) without altering the rhythm and the tempo.

Young horses tend not to balance their weight under the rider by moving their hind legs further under their bodies

Each extended tempo requires an increased impulsion and engagement of the hindquarters. This means that prior to asking for the extension, we need to build up power and impulsion, respectively. We prepare each increase in impulsion thoroughly by means of several half-halts. Then we send the horse "on its journey" packed with impulsion and energy. The horse should have the opportunity to place its hind legs further under its body, and it needs more space, so remember the *light seat bones and muscles*.

During the increase of impulsion, we sit as lightly as we possibly can. If we manage to open the overall shoulder joint during the increased impulsion, we can feel exactly how much tension flexes back from the reins, and we can maintain a light, flexible connection.

However, if we loosen the reins at the start of the increased impulsion, known as "throwing the reins away," the horse will lose its balance and, figuratively speaking, will fall on its nose.

The ongoing dispute with the cowboy hat. This "full-halt" can be observed at every practising area of a show, if a wind is blowing.

Seeing how difficult it is to increase the impulsion, it is even more difficult to reduce the impulsion and speed, in other words, to change to a lower gear. Doing this, it is important to ensure that the horse engages its hindquarters and shifts its weight further back, without pulling on the reins. The motto, therefore, is to ride forwards if we want to *slow down* – this is a strange concept, which we need to get used to.

If we want to halt our horse, irrespective of the pace it is currently moving at, this lesson is called the *full-halt*. According to mathematical rules, two half-halts should make a full-halt, but this does not apply to horses.

In certain circumstances, we may need four or even five half-halts to accomplish a correct full-halt.

The end of a full-halt is the final formation. This should not look like or bear any resemblance to a handstand. Instead, all four legs of the horse should be standing in a closed position, four-square. We can only achieve this if we monitor the hindquarters of our horse.

The temptation to leave one leg behind or to place it sideways is simply enormous – after all, we like our creature comforts as well.

The light seat bones and muscles should be applied during the full-halt to enable the horse to use its back without any load. After all, it is required to fully engage its hindquarters.

Exercise 21:
Full-halt

On the ball with reins: Prepare this exercise by means of a few half-halts, see Exercise 20.
If you find that your horse is engaging its hindquarters and placing its feet further under its body, shifting more of

Exercise 21: Full-halt.

its weight to the back, and becoming distinctly slower, then both calves should remain in contact with the horse's sides during the final swing, because you need to ensure that the horse brings all its legs together for the final formation. During the final swing, close your hands once more very quickly and then immediately relax them again.

In difficult situations, if for example other horses are rushing past you out of control, then you can augment your hand signals with a leg aid.

Interrupt the swinging in motion with the movement of the horse for a very short moment by closing your upper thighs on their inside. Every well-trained horse understands this braking signal.

Then immediately sit back lightly and in a relaxed way and swing in harmony with the horse. Even if you are sitting on a mule that has disguised itself as a riding horse, the braking movement with the legs is quite helpful. One should try to avoid getting involved in a tug-of-war.

16

The everyday and the rider's turn

"Bending the horse serves to increase its suppleness and thereby its dexterity, as well as to eliminate any stiffness." (Podhajsky)

Many hobby riders have a hard time during the winter months. They either freeze, hacking out in arctic temperatures, or if they are lucky enough to be able to use an indoor riding school, they battle their way through the unpopular school figures. Their antipathy is understandable because using the seat they use to ride straight lines leaves them fairly helpless when it comes to riding bends and circles. They bluff their way through the corners of the riding arena, but when it comes to circles, serpentines, or voltes, the result of their efforts will simply be a crooked horse's neck, an unwilling horse, and a dissatisfied riding instructor.

With the exception of the neck, which is much too willing to bend, the horse's spine

is a rather rigid construction. This mobility in the area of the neck is quite a problem, especially for novice and weaker riders, as the bending of the neck easily deceives them and they assume that this corkscrew twist means that the horse is already bending correctly.

If, on the other hand, we try to bend a horse correctly in the middle section of its spine, the constant work of the back and abdominal muscles is joined by the contraction of the inner side and the extension of the outer side – short and fat horses find this especially difficult to do.

The spine shows a certain mobility in the area leading to the lumbar vertebrae, before it becomes completely immobile in the rear area of the croup, the section before the dock.

When we are riding a turn, we request our horse to place both of its back legs

evenly under its body. The inner hind leg has the shorter way but needs to bend further and has to bear the weight. The outer hind leg must not step out sideways or drag behind.

All of this is strenuous, and our horse will not offer these movements voluntarily. If we *sit at a bend* when riding a turn, we imperatively expect the horse to also bend its spine slightly.

Making the horse bend its spine helps us to get through to its hindquarters and can encourage them to take up more weight. In a turn, we usually first drive the inside leg under the horse, and then try to gain control of the outside hind leg. For safety's sake, however, we change the rein to begin the game anew on the other rein. Once we have managed to drive both legs evenly underneath the centre of gravity, our efforts will have been successful; we have now lessened the weight on the forehand. Now our horse is in balance, and it is a pleasure to sit on it and control it.

Riding figures in the arena, therefore, is not a system of ingenious malevolence, but instead a gymnastic programme for horses. The bending on the part of the horse as well as the increased engagement of the hindquarters and the transfer of the weight from the forehand are strenuous, and therefore every horse attempts to evade this work. The

Julia is able to learn the bending seat as a complete movement, unlike the adults – what an enviable talent.

favorite pastime of horses is grazing, and they don't care a hoot whether the gymnastic work is healthy for them.

The natural bend to one side means that even on straight lines the horse likes to place one hind leg – usually the right one – slightly to the outside and supports itself on the diagonal shoulder to maintain its balance. In turns and circles this natural bend is even more noticeably unpleasant. Every horse will use these errors without inhibition and with great creativity, in order to evade the hated bend. The hind legs are placed outside the correct line, are twisted, dragged behind, or stepped unevenly.

If we can sit in a bend, we can cope with all these difficulties. For this purpose, however, we first need to learn new movements and, in addition, to apply in a modified way movements we have already learned. We will need:

- a special type of turning: the rider's turn
- a broad extension on the outside
- a changed swinging in harmony during the turn.

The large circle requires a slight bend; the small volte (six metres; in diameter) represents the highest level of a turn.

Parts of these two circles can be found in all figures, for example, in the small and large serpentines. When riding through a corner of the arena correctly, we are riding a partial volte. If the horse bends in the turn, this means that the forehand and the hindquarters are on different parts of a circle. Our seat is responsible for the hindquarters, and our upper body monitors the forehand of the horse, as Müseler stated the classic demand:

"With his hips, the rider needs to remain parallel to the hips of the horse and with his shoulders parallel to the shoulders of the horse."

The upper and lower body of the rider thereby turn in different directions during the turn. That means that the rider's body needs to turn somehow and somewhere. The important question is: how and where!

The everyday turn: If we sit on a chair, not thinking about riding, and turn to one side, we begin the turn with the head, take the inner shoulder with us into the turn, but leave the outer shoulder hanging fairly neglected. In this turn, we usually only put weight on one side of our buttocks as well – usually the inner side – the other seat bone is often even lifted up slightly. This normal type of daily turning has become so natural for us that each rider will initially try to turn in this manner when he is riding a turn on a horse. This has the following negative effects:

- If we begin the turn leading with the inner shoulder, the head of the horse will be pulled inward by the respective inside rein. That means that the hind leg on the same side loses impulsion through the braking effect and is no longer able to stretch under the horse's body to carry its weight.

Dagmar very distinctly in the bending seat to the right.

- If we sit in the saddle with our weight distributed solely on one seat bone and lift the other seat bone up, we lose all control over the outer hind leg. An old saying reminds us: "When the cat's away, the mice will play."

- If we twist ourselves in a corkscrew fashion or give way in the hip, we will be unable to open our hip joints sufficiently. The swinging of the pelvis in harmony with the horse is impeded, the inside calf presses forcefully against the horse's side

Dagmar very distinctly in the bending to seat to the left.

and can no longer be applied in a forward massaging motion. The rider's outside calf slips forwards and thereby loses control of the outer hind leg of the horse.

We normally execute all rotations of the body with the slanted (usually outer layer) of muscles which cover our entire body. The corkscrew-like rotation started by the head is completely impractical when sitting on the horse.

Therefore, we need to find a different kind of turning.

*Exercise 22: The rider's turn:
pull yourself in the new direction.*

Stay completely straight and do not fold in any part. Pull yourself into the new direction in the lower abdomen with an upright upper body and relaxed straight shoulders. Make sure that both seat bones remain completely unchanged in their position on the ball.

Can you still remember how difficult it was for you to make the lower straight muscles work for you? Now you will have the same problem. If they do not have the strength to begin the turn in the lower abdomen, many riders can only manage a distortion of the upper body as a substitute action, which is, of course, completely useless.

Only the rider's turn complete with the bending seat allows us to have an influence on the hindquarters and the forehand of the horse, as well as all its legs, which want to step out of line and need to be brought back into position.

Naturally, the horse is not too happy with this and will attempt to remove us from our supreme position with a bag full of tricks. This usually happens at the beginning of a riding lesson. If the horse is still stiff and cannot really engage the inside hind leg to carry its weight, it will try to place us onto the outside seat bone in every turn. At this moment, the inner side of the horse is still higher than the outside, and slipping outward like this happens all too easily, be-

Exercise 22:
The Rider's Turn

On the ball: Sit correctly in an upright posture, the thoracic girdle and head in balance. Your feet have complete contact with the floor. Hold arms and hands as if you were holding a pair of reins. The lower abdomen has inner as well as outer slanted abdominal muscles. Here, in the lowest possible part of the body, you will have to try to start a small turn in the required direction with the help of this group of muscles.

Correct bend of the carriage horse through schooling by the rider.

cause during this stage we will definitely be sitting uncomfortably and in an unstable position. The horse will push us out of balance bit by bit, either by means of gentle shoving, or by a distinct rising of the inner side, until we only put weight on the outer seat bone and sit completely unevenly on one side.

We can counter this persistent shifting of our seat with the same method. We need to move back onto the inner seat bone, or to use a better term, pull ourselves back with the help of the slanted muscles of the lower abdomen.

The forehand is controlled by the reins, in other words, by our shoulders. The outside rein monitors a difficult partner: the outside foreleg. If we lose contact here or pull on the inside rein with the other hand, the horse will "drop over its shoulder."

This technical term means that the horse places its outside foreleg out of line and, in this way for the sake of a change, evades the turning movement.

17

Good extension
is the way to bending

In the bend, our outer seat bone and outer leg control the outer hind leg of the horse, which is prone to step out of line. The technical term for this leg position is called *restraining,* and only very few riders make an effort to try to understand the deeper meaning of this word, or much less struggle to perform it. The top rider *Lindenbauer*, one of the best riders and teachers at the Spanish Riding School in Vienna, once said:

"Anybody who can ride a correct turn, will be able to manage everything else."

Although the rider's turn is an important part of the bending seat, it and the driving inside calf alone cannot bend the horse. The restraining outer calf also plays its part!

During the turn, the outer part of the horse is longer than the inner side which is pushed together. This means for the rider that his outside hip joint as well as the leg also has to follow this extension.

As the hip joint and the leg cannot change themselves, this extension is carried out in the base area of the leg, in the groin region, the area where strong ligaments and tendons give our legs stability.

Unfortunately, the extension is not a stable thing. On the contrary, we lose quite a large amount of it with every movement the horse makes. Therefore, we will have to extend the leg again and again, or increase the extension, in rhythm with the swinging movement.

Exercise 23:
The Extension

On a chair and the ball: Sit in a correct upright posture, the thoracic girdle and head in balance. Now stretch one slightly angled leg fairly far back. The seat and the leg must not tense up in any way. Don't lift the leg up unilaterally; both seat bones should always bear the weight equally. Place your hands under your buttocks and check this. You will feel a slight pull in the groin area – that is normal. The stretched-back leg maintains complete contact with the floor through the sole of the foot.

Now try to lessen the tension that is created by the strong extension and after that also try to relax the leg overall. Change the leg. You will find that again you have a side that performs the exercise more easily – that is the problem with riding. We are distinctly right-handed or left-handed, as well as right-footed or left-footed. Our horse has the same problem and is markedly more dextrous on one side.

Exercise 23: The extension.

How much we have to extend depends to a large degree on the shape of our horse. If we are riding a well-nourished, round-bellied horse, we will need to extend very far and relax our entire hip muscles very consciously.

Jantar is cheating and only bends his neck, instead of following the bend through the entire body.

He places Katharina completely twisted to one side and she is pressing hard with her left leg.

Now she manages to bend him through the body slightly...

...and immediately sits with relaxed legs against the horse's sides.

Exercise 24: Sitting in a bending position: Pull yourself into the new direction and turn the inside of the outer upper thigh.

Exercise 24:
Sitting in a Bending Position

On the ball: Sit correctly in an upright posture, the thoracic girdle and head in balance. Your feet have complete contact with the floor. Hold arms and hands in the riding position.

Start the rider's turn in a slanting position of the lower abdomen. At the same time, distinctly extend the base area of the outer leg, in other words, the inside of the upper thigh. This ensures that the outer calf automatically slips back and the knees open up slightly.

At the same time, your upper body remains straight and upright and, with relaxed and straight shoulders, swings slightly to the inside through the rider's turn. Both seat bones remain evenly on the ball.

On the horse, at this moment your hands will take the horse's head with you to the inside, with an even, flexible connection of the reins.

If somebody is willing to play "Horse" for you, you can also practise the bending seat with the rein connection.

Now imagine that the ball is a living, breathing creature that has the same extension problems as you do. Become very light in the seat and keep your outer thigh on the ball. It should remain completely relaxed, despite the extension. The horse should bend itself around the inside calf: however, it will only do this as long as it is not impeded by a hard, tensed up and pinching upper inner thigh. In other words; keep this part of your leg completely relaxed as well.

During the bend, the inside hind leg of the horse has less ground to cover than normal, but it has to bend itself more, carrying additional weight and therefore lifting up with even more intensive impulsion. As your horse will not voluntarily carry out such additional work itself, we will need more than just the seat aids. We will also need the inner calf. However, we must not press and squeeze it, or bang it against the horse's side. Instead, in harmony with the swinging rhythm, we will rotate it from the back, gently massaging it against the horse's side. When riding a bend, the outside calf, instead of doing the hard work, simply needs to be present. It will become increasingly active if the outer hind leg of the horse tries to escape sideways or simply drags along and needs encouragement. The outside calf helps the outside seat bone, by distinctly rotating along the horse's side in rhythm with the horse's movement. If the horse subsequently conducts itself properly, the calf, lying lightly against the horse, can go back to "breathing" with the horse's side.

Now imagine that you yourself were a horse and, in the truest sense of the word, a "bit carrier." Having a lot of metal in your mouth is not a very happy situation in itself. Imagine how disagreeable it must be if these metal bits are unilaterally pulled through the mouth unannounced, every time you perform a change of direction!

If, on the other hand, the seat of the rider clearly announces the turn, and the horse's head and shoulders are introduced into the turn with an even and flexible connection with both hands, the horse's life immediately becomes far more agreeable.

18

When the circle changes to an ellipse

Taking up the rider's turn and the outside turn, we have placed ourselves in a distinct bending position, but we are still completely immobile – a statue of a rider.

This means that the movements of the horse are maintained during the turn, so that we will also be able to apply our proven swinging motions here. The extension on the outside, however, will "extend" our swinging circle in such a way that the circle becomes an ellipse. On the outside we therefore swing like the shape of a flat ellipse.

Our outside leg is already lying slightly behind the girth, and by means of the wide elliptical shaped swinging back of the hip, which at the same time means a sinking back of the leg, we are able to "take hold of" and/or monitor the horse's outside hind leg particularly well.

During the bend, we will need a high degree of dynamics on the inside – much higher steps. Therefore, we swing in the form of a standing ellipse on the inside. This trick allows us to swing alternately on the inside and the outside in the same rhythm and also combine the outside extension with increased activity on the inside.

If we want to swing with particular efficiency, which is the case on the inside if we are riding a turn, we particularly need to activate the pelvic swing in that area. The bending motion in our lower abdomen results in the straight abdominal muscles feeling slightly impaired, and they cannot carry out the difficult job of the bending swing on their own. What remedy do we have? The inner slanted muscles of the lower abdomen help out in this case. We

96

therefore use these slanted muscles in two ways: on the one hand for the turn and on the other as a support for the swinging action.

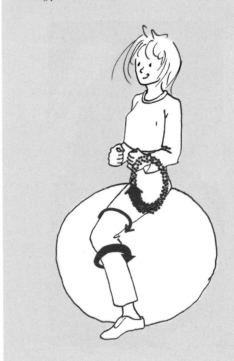

Exercise 25: Swinging in a left-rein bend on the inside of the body. The inner pelvis is swinging actively, and the lower leg presses in.

Exercise 25:
Swinging in a Bend on the Inside

On the ball: Sit correctly in an upright posture, the thoracic girdle and head in balance. Your feet have complete contact with the floor. Hold arms and hands in the riding position.

Start the rider's turn by slanting the lower abdomen. At the same time, extend the base area of the outer leg, automatically leading to the outside thigh slipping back.

Now swing consciously, dynamically, and demandingly on the inside, as if tracing the shape of a standing (i.e., vertical) ellipse. This means increasing the lower part of the swinging motion, the forward movement, and pulling emphatically upward by means of a particularly active *thoracic girdle*. You will have to be "ready for takeoff" from the start, because you will only be able to get the horse to move with more active, springing steps. Also rotate your lower leg and massage the tight calf muscle against the horse's side in rhythm with the horse's movement at the moment of the emphasized forwards-upwards swinging motion. Then release the calf immediately.

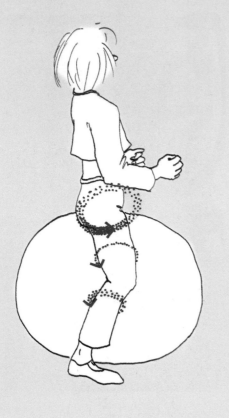

Exercise 26: Swinging in a left-rein bend on the outside of the body. At the same time extend the inside of the outer thigh.

and consciously let the outer hip joint slip downward to the rear.

Emphasize the extension and the part of the swinging motion that is moving backwards, the lowering motion. If your horse continues quietly and secretly to try to back out its outer hind leg, catch the culprit with a distinct forwards movement.

In other words, start by extending and lowering then use the active pelvic swing in the lower part of the ellipse – emphasize the forward drive. For this purpose, rotate the lower leg, which usually only lies against the horse's side to monitor its movements, with tightened calf toward the horse's side. Then release the calf again immediately and start from the beginning.

We now try for the full Monty: the bilateral, simultaneous swinging motion in the turn. If you can manage to execute this complicated combination of movements even marginally, you have reached the right "rider's path."

Exercise 26:
Swinging in a Bend on the Outside

On the ball: Sit as above. The outer side of the horse has become longer through the bend and you should adapt to it. Therefore, swing in the shape of a lying (i.e., horizontal) ellipse. Extend the base area of the leg on the outside,

Exercise 27:
Swinging in a Bend on the Inside and Outside

On the ball: Sit correctly in an upright posture, the thoracic girdle and head in

Wrong rider's outer leg during the bend: the upper thigh is not stretched at its starting position; the outer seat bone lifts up; and the lower leg is pulled up to the croup at an acute angle.

Correct rider's outer leg during the bend. The upper leg is stretched at the starting position; both seat bones stay on the horse; the lower legs hang loosely behind the girth.

Incorrect rider's inner leg during the bend: upper thigh bends outward; the back upper thigh muscles and the lower leg are pressed against the horse's sides with some force – the horse stiffens and refuses to bend.

balance. Your feet have complete contact with the floor. Hold arms and hands in the riding position.

Start the rider's turn in a slanting position in the lower abdomen. At the same time, extend the base area of the outer leg, automatically leading to the outside thigh slipping back.

Combine the two swinging movements, in other words, the inside standing ellipse with the forwards-upward swing, with the outside lying ellipse with the extension and lowering motion.

Make sure that you swing on the inside and the outside alternately, in the same rhythm.

Remember that you will have a favourite side even when swinging in the bend, and therefore always change the bend from one side to the other and back.

Correct rider's inner leg during the bend: the upper thigh lies gently and softly
– and the horse will bend in response to this fine inner leg.

Whether you make lateral movements, turning on the haunches, or pirouettes, all these movements depend on perfect bending and are not that difficult to ride once you have accomplished this extremely difficult lesson.

Unfortunately it is also true that every horse will always try to evade bending exercises and therefore make life difficult for the rider.

What do you do when you have the feeling of sitting on an iron crossbeam, helpless and without any means of control? What you do is control your seat! The horse will already have the upper hand if it has managed to shift the rider to the outside seat bone, and weaker riders unfortunately react by sitting crookedly, or they bend in the hip or waistline to seemingly get back into balance – which they will be unable to achieve in this way. Once the seat and balance are lost, only the legs can get hold of the horse's movements – the clinging monkey is back in full force, and there is not even a hint of bending.

If, on the other hand, you remain imperturbable in an upright posture and always move back with your seat onto this stiff, pushing inner hind leg and patiently drive it bending and swinging under the horse's center of balance until it can take over the rider's weight with impulsion – then you will rarely get a chance to make yourself comfortable! Alternatively, if the clever horse has won the battle and is beginning to practice the splits with its freed hind leg, it will have to support itself on the diagonal rein, so as not to fall on its nose.

In the moment when a soft and flexible connection is no longer discernible, even the weaker rider should notice that he is now only sitting on a "three-legged" horse. In this situation only one thing can help: correct the seat and start off anew.

Drive the above-mentioned leg as the inside leg under the horse's body by means of an energetic bending and swinging motion, but on no account pull the horse around by the reins, as it is impossible to regain lost hind legs with the reins.

A final step – the canter

De la Guérinière said of the medium school-ing canter:

"During this movement the horse should, so to speak, spring with impulsion in all joints and captivate the onlooker as well as its rider through its beauty."

The first exercises at the canter certainly won't succeed quite as perfectly. The better the horse is being ridden, the more it will engage its hindquarters and carry its own weight, and the more pleasant its strides will be. In riding schools, novices will rarely be allocated sensitive and well-schooled horses. This means that in addition to having to cope with their own balancing problems, they will also have to become acquainted with an unpleasant bumpy canterer of a riding school horse.

If you try riding a horse forward in a straight line, you will soon realize that horses become even more crooked at this pace. The hind end can disengage to the out-side as well as to the inside. The only thing the croup will rarely be is straight.

The sequence of footfalls at the canter:

First phase:
The outside hind leg leaves the ground.
Second phase:
Diagonal pair of legs touch the ground.
Third phase:
The inside foreleg touches the ground.
Moment of suspension:
All four legs are in the air.

The canter is not a striding but a jumping pace, and therefore far more dynamic than the walk and trot. If the hindquarters disen-

Canter on the left rein, phase one:
the right outside hind leg leaves the ground.

Canter on the left rein, phase two:
the diagonal pair of legs touch the ground.

gage to one side at a crooked canter, the rider will sit very uncomfortably. Here, the rider sits on an ejector seat, with precious little influence. He can only hope that the horse won't take advantage of the situation.

However; even the old equestrian masters of the past knew how to help themselves. Bending was the solution! Controlling the inner as well as the outer leg constantly and encouraging the hindquarters to engage is only possible in a bend. That means that we cannot use the round swinging circles which we apply at the walk and trot in straight lines. We need to sit in the bending posture at all times, in other words, swing in elliptical shapes, even when we want to canter forward in a straight line.

Each individual phase at the canter conveys four different positions and feelings of the seat in rapid sequence. The only phase we can recognize is the second phase where the diagonal pair of legs touch the ground – this conveys a feeling of the deep relaxed seat. All other phases not only push us high up, as well as up and down crookedly, but we also receive a forwards or backwards jolt, and at the same time one area of the horse's back is lifted and then lowered and lifted again accordingly, with a considerable difference between the two levels.

As if it is not enough that all hell has broken loose under our buttocks, our horse now also needs more sufficient freedom of the reins than ever before. Where is that feeling of pure bliss that *De la Guérinière* enthused about?

Canter on the left rein, phase three:
the inside left foreleg touches the ground.

Canter on the left rein, phase four:
moment of suspension.

The problem at the canter is not the learning of a new movement – we are already acquainted with all of the riding movements – but once more our inability to loosen up. With the exception of the diagonal second phase, the horse has only one foot on the ground, and during the moment of suspension not even that. This means that we suddenly have to cope with immense shifts in the centre of gravity, to which we have to react with corresponding speed. In addition to the sideways swerving of the horse's back, we now also have to contend with a rapidly changing up and down, similar to the movement of a rocking horse – a lot of riders have problems with this in combination with the constantly bending seat.

If the abdominal muscles were fully active and if the hip joint were to adjust to all these up-and-down movements right from the start, by means of a massive "overall opening programme," it would be easy to sit in balance at the canter. If the rider, however, clings on just the slightest bit due to a feeling of insecurity, it cannot function and the upper body begins to adopt a wobbling movement immediately. The more restless the upper body is, the less it is possible for the opening programme of the hip joint and the pelvic swing to function. Catch-22 comes into effect, and the clinging monkey is back.

To ask a novice rider to get a feeling for the four phases of a canter stride immediately, would be unrealistic. Even most experienced riders have problems with this.

The four phases of the canter:
Phase 1: the outside hind leg jumps under the horse's body carrying the weight of horse and rider; the other three legs don't touch the ground.

Phase 2: the inner hind leg and the outer foreleg touch the ground at the same time.

Phase 3: the inner foreleg touches the ground on its own.

Phase 4: moment of suspension – all four legs are in the air.

Let us first try to achieve a theoretical image of what happens under our buttocks during each stride. In time we can then find our way into this pace sitting on the horse, learning to control and improve the strides.

During each canter stride of the horse, we swing in a complete ellipse, alternating between the inside and the outside; all four phases of the canter stride are contained in this ellipse.

Naturally, the ellipses are different again due to the bending: standing upright on the inside, in order to drive the inside hind leg of the horse forward with impulsion, and on the outside lying horizontal so that the horse has a chance to extend itself with ease and comfort.

First phase

– the yardstick for the quality of the canter:

If the outside hind leg touches the ground well underneath the weight of the horse, transfers weight onto its hindquarters to carry it, and strikes off energetically and with impulsion, then we have a first-class, flexible canter – very much in the sense of De la Guérinière. If, on the other hand, the dragging outside hind leg can only manage a tired, crooked, and limp hop, the rider will slowly "starve" to oblivion during this lifeless canter.

We can only engage a lacklustre outside hind leg by means of particularly energetic forward impulsion. The outside calf, which normally only "breathes" gently with the horse's side, needs to be fully activated and rotate toward the side of the horse with a tight calf muscle. If our horse decides it still can't understand, we can also make our intentions clear with a small touch with the spur: "Wake up my friend, this is not the time to fall asleep!"

Second phase

– the comfortable one:

Now we are sitting very comfortably, as we have arrived at the lowest, most relaxed point of our stride. In this phase, we engage the inside hind leg to carry the weight.

Third phase

– the uncomfortable one:

The inside front leg alone touches the ground far ahead, which creates great demands on our balance. A forceful push comes from behind. We are lifted out of our deep, stable seat, and to top it all, the horse's back is now moving downhill.

Now in particular, the horse will require even more rein to allow it the considerable freedom to nod its head – how can we cope with all that? Quite easily: we collect all the courage we have and open the hip joint, and the shoulder joint, at the same time. The rider's work at the canter is in no way restricted to engaging the horse's hindquarters and driving them beneath the horse, but in phases three and four, we will have to loosen up the hip joint *extremely* wide, irrespective of our problems with keeping our balance. If we only sit on the horse, scared and without doing anything, we will soon automatically change back into a clinging monkey. Then the horse will feel impaired; it will canter without impulsion and expressiveness. This is also called "riding the horse into the ground."

Due to the dynamic of the strides, the overall opening of the shoulders needs to be carried out particularly actively, to ensure that our arms can swing with the movement of the horse's head in gentle contact with its mouth.

Fourth phase

– the moment of suspension:

Now the horse has lifted all four hooves into the air. This phase does not give the rider an ideal feeling of the seat and riding. But in this phase, in particular, we have to allow the horse a particularly large degree of space and freedom of movement by lightening the seat bones and muscles. After all, it is just preparing to arrange all its legs in the correct position for the next stride.

This moment of suspension is the moment when the horse sorts out its legs completely anew, when asked for a flying change of the rein at the canter, for example, from the left to the right rein. It should go without saying that the horse does not want to be disturbed by the rider. Each riding discipline uses slightly different signals to tell the horse distinctly what we want it to do. The Western rider, for example, transfers his weight slightly to the outside, and may also bend his horse slightly to the outside and use his outside calf on the saddle girth. As these signals are very clear, the horse will probably strike out into the correct canter. Bending, straightening the horse, or impulsion will be less important.

Our riding discipline may be difficult to learn, but will allow more room for development later on.

The bending position causes our outside calf to shift backwards, which also gives the horse a certain signal effect. However, we "start" our canter by means of an increased forwards and upwards swinging motion of the inner hip and remain in balance all the time.

It is not enough that our horse changes pace to a canter; we also want this to happen with impulsion and with a correct bend. Therefore, the correct striking out at the canter in itself is already a fairly exacting lesson.

Exercise 28a: Outside view of striking out at the canter on the left rein.

Exercise 28b: Inside view of striking out at the canter on the left rein by means of a particularly active pelvic swing.

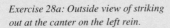

Exercise 28:
Striking Out at the Canter

On the ball: Sit correctly in an upright posture, the thoracic girdle and head in balance. Your feet have complete contact with the floor. Hold arms and hands in the riding position. Alert the horse to the fact that you want it to canter by taking up the bending posture.

Start the rider's turn in a slanting position of the lower abdomen and "lead" the forehand of the horse to the inside with both hands. At the same time, distinctly extend the base area of the outer leg, in other words, the inside of the upper thigh.

This ensures that the outer calf automatically slips back; however, do not interrupt the rhythm of swinging with the motion. The swinging circles turn into swinging ellipses. Check the horse's outside hind leg! If necessary, engage it more fully with an increased forwards swinging in the lower part of the ellipse and at the same time rotate the outside calf against the horse's side. At this point, and not before, give the horse the final command to strike out at the canter.

For this purpose it is important to emphasize the inside lower part of the standing ellipse by means of a particularly active pelvic swing. Your horse will strike out in an energetic canter – almost as *de la Guérinière* described it.

If a rider has a "hand-brake," in other words, a blocked shoulder joint, striking out at the canter cannot function properly because even at the first stride, the horse has insufficient freedom of movement of the reins. He will thus continue to canter, not with expressive swinging strides, but rather hopping around like a rabbit.

The terms "canter on the left rein" and "canter on the right rein" do not indicate the direction in which the rider and horse ride, but only tell which front leg is leading, i.e., places its hoof on the ground in the third phase. If we give the wrong aid at the canter, ride with the horse bent to the outside, or displace our weight to the outside, our horse will strike out at the canter, but we can feel that something is wrong. "Wrong rein!" is the instructor's reproof. At the same time, the experienced rider shines, seemingly doing the same

thing, but in his case, the "incorrect" canter is called the counter-canter. Seems a bit confusing, does it not?

Counter-canter movements serve predominantly as corrective aids and are not suitable for us at the present. The counter-canter helps improve collection and corrects the natural bend to one side. All movements at the counter-canter are particularly tiring for the horse in the turns and should only be ridden for short periods and with the correct collection. Otherwise, this could lead to damage to the tendons and ligaments.

Exercise 29:
The Canter

On the ball: If your horse strikes out as described in Exercise 28, you will need to do all you can to maintain the impulsion and the dynamic of the strides.

For this purpose you have to animate both hind legs, if not in fact engage them during every stride. At the same time you will have to loosen up your hip and shoulder joints overall and in extreme form.

You always "engage" the outside hind leg during the moment of swinging backwards and lowering down. In addition, you may have to rotate the outer calf from behind onto the horse's side. This is phase one of the canter stride.

In Western riding the canter phase should be round, but not in an upward motion.

Immediately afterwards – almost following on and combining, you encourage the inside hind leg by means of an increased pelvic swing.

At the same time emphasize the bottom part of the standing ellipse as well as the upward part.

Also at the same time, rotate the tight muscle of the inside calf against the horse's side – this is part two of the canter stride.

Then, in phases three and four, you just have to loosen up your shoulder and hip joints and circle and also loosen up all other joints such as the elbow and wrist, knee and ankle, and flex your legs in the stirrups. Then you start once more with phase one, the activation of the outside hind leg. You will find that you have a favourite side at the canter as well. Therefore, always practise on both reins.

"You are not the one who is supposed to canter: leave it to the horse!" a rider will be reprimanded who tries to push his horse going at a lifeless canter by the pumping action of his upper body. He will not succeed, because he is clinging on and blocking at the same time.

"Don't push your horse backwards, drive it forwards at the canter!" This rider again pushes because he obviously cannot cope with his abdominal muscles. He sits at the back of the saddle with a hollowed out back. The heels are pulled up; the knees are clinging on; the upper back is rounded; the shoulders are falling forwards, hands ramrod-stiff hands – it is all visible now, because the canter feels rather dangerous to begin with. There is only one remedy for this: the iron determination not to give in to these strides, but rather to act irrationally: I always relax when the going is at its least comfortable! Whoever can change this philosophy into action and whoever manages in phase one and two to engage the hind legs of his horse and manages to stay upright and relaxed in the third and fourth phase despite all hardship will soon be on track to the pleasure described by de la Guérinière.

When out hacking, you should not sit at the canter but instead adopt the forward seat with shortened stirrup leathers. The rider's weight rests increasingly in the stirrups, so that the rider stands more than he sits. Basically, it does not matter whether you ride out cantering on the right rein or the left. It is only important that you change the rein from time to time, even if the horse offers you its better side time and time again.

Freedom of the back – the forward seat – jumping

At the walk, the rider always sits down in the saddle. At the trot or canter, however, the only place where the rider sits down is in the riding arena. Out on a hack, where the going can be rough, a mixture of sitting down and standing is adopted, which lightens the horse's back and allows it more freedom of movement.

The rising trot was invented in England. On the continent, the rider sat down at the trot and also at the canter. Only toward the end of the nineteenth century, when the French and Prussians finally also realized what advantages this "revolutionary riding discipline," as it was called at the time, had, especially going across country, was it added to the military education.

Berlatan de Nemethy, a well-known instructor, described the rising trot thus: *"No sudden abrupt rise into the air and*

back into the saddle, but a gentle swinging upwards and forwards." Despite that, even in those days as well as today, there were and are uncounted faulty interpretations: the "Up and flop riders." These specialists pull themselves up with a pull and keep a firm grasp on the reins. Then their feet slip away forwards, they lose their balance and with their entire weight fall back into the saddle with a mighty thump at the next stride. In order to protect themselves from this exceedingly painful thumping, the horses tense up their back muscles to an extreme, which isn't a healthy thing, of course – not a very considerate or relieving riding style.

At the trot, the two sides of the horse's back are lifted and lowered in turn at every stride. If we are riding the correct *rising trot*, we flex slightly in the stirrups every

When you hack out, always let your horse walk on a loose rein – except in dangerous moments –
or do you want to school your horse to move at a pass?

time we are lifted up by the horse's movement. We also increase the upward part of
a swinging circle with our abdominal
muscles far enough so that we are no longer in the saddle at the next beat, but instead are "floating" above the saddle. We

Exercise 30: The rising trot.

down in the saddle. We swing with the horse's movements, and we sit in a bending way when riding turns.

Exercise 30:
The Rising Trot

On the ball: Sit correctly in an upright posture, with the thoracic girdle and head in balance. Your feet have complete contact with the floor. Hold your arms and hands in the riding position. Swing at the trot.

Now increase the upward part of a swinging circle by means of a particularly active pelvic swing. You will rise slightly up from the ball. Then loosen up and at the same time slide gently back onto the ball. The next active pelvic swing follows immediately.

then gently slide back into the saddle at the next beat. Due to the fact that we do not actually stand up but only lift our buttocks slightly, we cannot sit down heavily – everything is just a swinging motion: "gentle swinging up and forwards."

The following applies to all riding styles that relieve the horse's back: the rider *rides in exactly the same way as he would, sitting*

When out hacking, it does not matter on which leg you begin the trot. The only important thing is that you change over and back again repeatedly, in order to ensure you do not strain just one diagonal pair of legs by sitting down on it all the time. Changing the rein is accomplished by sitting out an extra beat.

It is far more difficult to ride on the so-called "correct" leg in the riding arena. In Austria and Germany, the novice riders look down anxiously to the outer front leg of the

If you also want to jump out on a hack, you should shorten your stirrup leathers by three or four holes.

horse. If it swings forward, the rider needs to "swing in harmony," which relieves the inside back leg.

In England, however, the rider rides exactly opposite.

At the beginning of a riding lesson, we first loosen up the horse, which will be stiff from standing in the stable, by initially walking on a loose rein and then by riding at the rising trot. For this we naturally retain the normal length of our stirrup leathers.

When going out on a hack, however, we shorten the leathers by approximately two holes. If we intend to jump also, or to ride up and down steep slopes, we can shorten the leathers by three or even four holes.

We need the *forward seat* for jumping as well as for difficult terrain on a hack. *"The rider canters, climbs and jumps with the forward seat. The upper body is folded forward to a larger or lesser degree, the buttocks are shifted backwards accordingly (balance). The centre of gravity of*

Exercise 31: The forward seat.

Exercise 31:
The Forward Seat

Standing: Stand with legs apart in a correct upright posture, the thoracic girdle and head in balance, arms and hands in the riding position. The normal, relaxed position of the knees no longer suffices – you need to bend them fairly sharply. Maintain full contact with the ground all the time! The lower you bend in the knees, the more your upper body leans forwards and the closer the elbows come to the thighs.

Transfer more weight to the balls of the feet – that is where your feet would be in the stirrups – take up a bending position and canter. In other words, swing around in the air and flex in the hip joints and in all other joints of the legs.

the rider thereby corresponds with that of the horse." (Müseler)

Now the moment has come when we have to say good-bye to the physio-ball and are able to imitate to a small degree riding situations in a standing posture.

The hip and knee joint need to absorb all movements in this constant standing situation.

When *climbing steep hills*, the hindquarters and back muscles of the horse work particularly actively. Therefore, we transfer our weight into the stirrups and stand in the forward seat with very low flexing heels, swinging joints, and a slightly forward-bent upper body. We provide the horse with complete freedom of the back and reins.

It makes a significant difference to the horse whether we only touch its sides with our lower legs and swing in the motion with all our joints, or whether we hold on

Exercise 31: The forward seat.

with our calves. If you experience problems maintaining balance, it is far more sensible not to cling onto the horse with your legs but rather to support yourself on both sides of the horse's neck with your hands – naturally with a loose rein. This ensures that the horse does not feel hindered.

We can also take hold of the middle section of the mane, which also gives us a feeling of safety and hardly impairs the horse in its freedom of movement.

When *climbing down steep hills*, our horse may engage its hindquarters even more than climbing uphill. Again, it requires complete freedom of the back. It also needs to be able to stretch its neck, to lift or lower it in order to maintain its balance better. This does not pose a problem in less steep surroundings. However, if the going is extreme …

If the hindquarters of the horse slip sideways in very steep country, the horse can lose its balance, slip down, or even fall. Therefore, the rider needs to keep his horse absolutely straight and ride down steep hills vertically. For this purpose, we once more transfer our full weight into the stirrups, with very low flexing heels, swinging joints, the upper body leaning slightly forward, and we give the horse complete freedom of its back. At the same time we need to make sure that our horse remains straight! This difficult task is undertaken by our calves, which lead and direct the horse without clinging to its sides, as well as the reins, which need to allow the horse freedom of the neck but still have to maintain contact – a tightrope walk!

High speed always transfers the centre of gravity of the horse forwards, which you can observe clearly on a racing track. The stirrups are extremely short and the rider leans his upper body forward accordingly. Contact with the saddle is lost almost completely – the constant high speed requires this. The conditions are completely different, however, for jumping.

"A good jump is dependent on the ability of the rider to ride the horse with the correct impulsion, speed and balance into the correct take-off zone.

The relationship of these three factors, impulsion, tempo, and balance can vary as such. The speed may be only moderate, provided the impulsion is forceful enough, and even the balance can be slightly lacking, if the combination of speed and impulsion is adapted to the fence to be jumped.

This means that the seat of the rider and his ability to influence the horse correctly are far more important in the approaching stage than his posture during the moment of suspension itself." (Steinkraus)

Riding between the fences is handled differently wherever you are. In Germany, for example, an almost normal sitting posture is preferred – naturally with shortened stirrup leathers. In England, on the other hand, the rider usually remains in the forward seat between the fences. At the take-off, however, each rider assumes the forward seat in order to allow the horse complete freedom of the back. The horse needs to have the chance to stretch itself in its particular way above the fence – the technical term for this is "bascule."

The rider should not only ride his horse at the required speed and with the necessary impulsion between the jumps, but also needs to have enough of a feeling of balance that he does not interfere with the horse during the take-off phase or the moment of suspension, any more than during the landing phase.

This "flying posture" of the rider staying with the horse during its movements – the adaptation of the human centre of balance to that of the horse – is often described as "snap-fold forward."

Exercise 32:
Jumping – Snap-fold Forward

Standing: Stand as in the above Exercise 31, adopt the forward seat and swing and flex at the canter.

Now the moment of the take-off arrives: at this moment, flex down in the hip and in the joints of the legs and not only open your hip joints overall, but also let your buttocks sink backwards in a relaxed manner.

The downward flexion of all your joints means that your upper body automatically bends forward a bit and you can allow the horse complete freedom of the reins.

Move back into an upright position and swing and flex again at the canter.

"Some experienced riders seem to have got the idea fixed firmly in their mind that it is necessary to 'do' something during the moment of take-off, as the horse jumps off the ground.

This tenacious idea is also a very damaging idea, as it is based on the prerequisite that the rider does something – or several things – at precisely the correct moment, something he does not have to do at all.

I also believed this for a long time as I could not believe that a horse could have the ability to jump off the ground without any – at least a very small 'aid' on my part.

'It is larger than you are – don't try to carry it, make sure that it carries you!' is a piece of advice which I will never forget again, after it was pointed out to me with increasing impatience by Morton (Cappy) Smith during a series of hot summer afternoons a few years ago.

Eventually, I understood and I am grateful to my instructor to this day that he drummed this sensible principle into my head.

To put it into clear words, the rider does absolutely nothing while the horse is jumping. I am convinced that nothing is necessary – not even a small relaxation or a bit of additional pressure with the calves.

If the posture of the rider is correct during the approach, in other words, if he is sitting in balance, the thrust of the horse that is preparing for the flight will automatically 'close' his seat." (Steinkraus).

William Steinkraus, himself a rider with an excellent style, was certainly right in his statement that a perfect posture during the approach results automatically in the correct posture during the moment of suspension.

But, let's be honest – who is perfect? Certainly not a novice rider. Jumping is always a bit exciting, and expectation often means tension and tight muscles.

However, a rider with tensed up muscles is just as disturbing for the horse as during dressage. You should therefore practise the

We now take our leave and hope that we have shown you how many things you can do correctly and incorrectly on a horse.

snap-fold movement, although the comfortable situation in the living room seems miles away from the dynamic jumping situation.

To round things off

We have now reached the end of the basic training. All more complicated lessons, for example, lateral movements, pirouettes, piaffe and passage, however advanced they sound, are based on the rider's movements that we learned in this book, and only represent refinements or new combinations of these rider's movements. Anybody who is hampered with basic faults will never be able to attain real improvements, either on a horse or in other sport categories.

Riding is a constant forwards and backwards. Every time our horse no longer moves forwards with impulsion, when movements no longer work out, it is time to *go back to the basics*! Only by returning to the correct basic work can we be saved, irrespective of whether we encounter resistance in dressage work, problems in show jumping or disobedience outside on a hack.

Once we have found the fault – which will have been caused almost always by ourselves – we can go forwards again in leaps and bounds, but we will soon encounter the next regression – that is all part of riding! Practise all the exercises until they have become second nature to you, because in critical situations you will not have the time to ponder, you can only react automatically to what you have learned. Once these movements have become so familiar that they are available to you in every situation, then riding will not only be great fun for you, but you will have also done a great deal for your own safety.

Do not expect that you will be able to carry out all the movements immediately once you are sitting on a horse. Even the most skilled riders had to work for years to develop a good seat in the saddle. Unfortunately you have chosen a fairly difficult sports discipline! Be happy instead about every improvement, however small it may be, because your horse will be happy with you. You have also chosen a wonderful sport, which you will be able to continue into old age. In riding, experience still counts – isn't that a wonderful thing?

I wish you successful practising!

Further reading

Bartle, Nicole.
Academic Equitation: A Training System Based on the Methods of D'Sure Baucher and L'Hotte.
Trafalgar Square, 2001.

De la Guérinière, François Robichon.
School of Horsemanship.
J A Allen & Co Ltd, 1993.

Feldenkrais, Moshe.
Awareness Through Movement: Easy-to-do Health Exercises to Improve Your Posture, Vision, Imagination, and Personal Awareness.
HarperCollins, 1991.

Loch, Sylvia.
The Classical Rider: Being at One with Your Horse.
J A Allen & Co Ltd, 1997.

Mairinger, Franz.
Horses Are Made to Be Horses.
John Wiley & Sons Inc., 2002.

Museler, Wilhelm et al.
Riding Logic.
Simon & Schuster, 1985.

Nelson, Hilda.
L'Hotte and the Quest for Lightness in Equitation.
J A Allen & Co Ltd, 1997.

Podhajsky, Alois.
The Complete Training of Horse and Rider in the Principles of Classical Horsemanship.
Bantam Doubleday Dell, 1967.

The Complete Training of Horse and Rider.
The Sportsman's Press, 1991.

Schusdziarra, Heinrich/Schudziarra, Volker.
An Anatomy of Riding.
Breakthrough Publications, 1985.

Seunig, Waldemar.
Essence of Horsemanship.
J A Allen & Co Ltd, 1984.

Steinkraus, William.
*Reflections on Riding and Jumping:
Winning Techniques for Serious Riders*.
Swan Hill Press, 1997.

Steinbrecht, G.
The Gymnasium of the Horse.
Xenophon Press, 1995.

… Riding and Jumping.
Pelham Books, 1971.

Swift, Sally.
Centred Riding.
Eburg Press, 1998.

von Dietze, Susanne.
*Balance in Movement: The Seat of the
Rider*.
J A Allen & Co Ltd, 1999.

Wätjen, Richard.
Dressage Riding.
J A Allen, 1988.

Many thanks

Many thanks also go to all the horse owners who let us use their horses for the photgraphs taken.

In particular, I would like to thank my two-legged and my four-legged models who endured all the perfidy of the weather and being photographed with friendly patience.

Angela Brunner

Dagmar Fischer

Judith Kremser

Klaus Möller

Eva Niessl

Manfred Niessl

Peter Prikler

Sabine Schmidt

Brigitte Sturm

Katharina Vokroj

HORSES:

ATLANTA

Owner: Peter Prikler

BILLY

Owner: Lydia Novacek

BODYGARD

Owner: Klaus Möller

DONNERWETTER

Owner: Judith Kremser

JANTAR

Owner: Andrea Prikler

NEW JACK CITY

Owner: Mike Baloun

ODETTE

Owner: Manfred Niessl

SOLITAIRE

Owner: Eva Niessl

TEMPTATION

Owner: Andera Prikler

The photographs for this book were shot in various riding schools; I would like to thank them for their friendly support:

MB-Trainigsstable, Sommerein

Neusiedler Csarda, Neusiedl am See

Reitklub Auwaldhof, Margartethen am Moss

Reitclub Edelseehof, Sarasdorf

Reitclub Schloss Trumau, Trumau

CADMOS
Equestrian

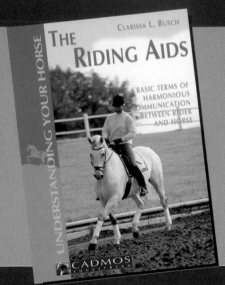

Clarissa L. Busch
THE RIDING AIDS

The riding aids are the medium through which the rider's wishes must be expressed. The author explains the elementary terms of the rider's aids in easily understood terms, starting with the relaxed, balanced seat which forms the basis of all riding. Natural aids using the weight of the body as well as legs and hands are initially explained individually, then shown in practical co-ordination: How do I bring my horse to a halt? How do I change from the trot to the walk, from the walk to the canter?

80 pages, paperback
ISBN 3-86127-905-3
£ 9,95

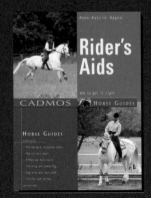

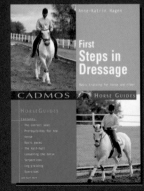

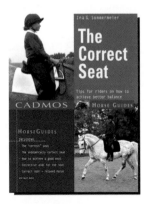

Anne-Katrin Hagen
RIDER'S AIDS

The rider's aids are the be-all and end-all of riding. Without them, no understanding or communication with the horse is possible. The aids must be conveyed to the horse both clearly and distinctly, and yet unobtrusively: as fine aids.
The author is a leading riding instructor and dressage trainer.

32 pages, paperback
ISBN 3-86127-942-8
£ 4,95

Anne-Katrin Hagen
FIRST STEPS IN DRESSAGE

Dressage involves drawing out the natural capability of the horse and shaping it into something beautiful and expressive. The horse must learn how to balance under the rider and move in elegant self-carriage.

32 pages, paperback
ISBN 3-86127-932-0
£ 4,95

Ina G. Sommermeier
THE CORRECT SEAT

In this guide the author describes, with the help of numerous exercises, how the rider can find his or her individual path to a balanced seat, to more delicate aids, and to a better communication with the horse.
Tips for riders on how to achieve better balance.

32 pages, paperback
ISBN 3-86127-933-9
£ 4,95

Cadmos Equestrian
171 GordonRoad   Nunhead
GB - London SE15 3RT
Tel.: 02074 504117   Fax: 08701 367219

CADMOS